Writing
CRITICALLY

Key Skills for
Post-Secondary Success

M. FELTHAM • WM. P. MEAHAN • W. HOTH

OXFORD
UNIVERSITY PRESS

OXFORD
UNIVERSITY PRESS

Oxford University Press is a department of the University of Oxford.
It furthers the University's objective of excellence in research, scholarship,
and education by publishing worldwide. Oxford is a registered trade mark of
Oxford University Press in the UK and in certain other countries.

Published in Canada by
Oxford University Press Canada
8 Sampson Mews, Suite 204,
Don Mills, Ontario M3C 0H5 Canada

www.oupcanada.com

Copyright © Oxford University Press Canada 2015

The moral rights of the author have been asserted

Database right Oxford University Press (maker)

Library and Archives Canada Cataloguing in Publication

Feltham, Mark, 1973- , author
Writing critically : key skills for post-secondary success / Mark
Feltham, Whitney Hoth, Wm. Paul Meahan.

Includes index.
ISBN 978-0-19-900680-9

1. English language—Rhetoric. 2. Academic writing. 3. Critical
thinking. I. Hoth, Whitney, author II. Meahan, Wm. Paul, author III. Title.

PE1408.F44 2015   808'.042   C2012-907241-9

Cover image: © Daryl Benson/Masterfile

Oxford University Press is committed to our environment.
This book is printed on Forest Stewardship Council® certified paper
and comes from responsible sources.

Printed and bound in Canada
1 2 3 4 — 18 17 16 15

Contents Overview

Contents

PART 2   Grammar, Mechanics, and Style

Introduction

This book is designed to help you improve your writing. You'll find a more detailed overview of its organization in Module 1.1, but the chart below provides an at-a-glance overview of book's structure.

Part 1: Critical Reading and Critical Response	Modules 1 through 9 in Part 1 take a step-by-step approach to help you develop your skills in numerous key areas of writing.
	If you review the table of contents, you'll see that we actually begin with a review of reading skills. We start here because college and university writing is usually about responding to assigned readings of various sorts.
	From there we move on to such topics as how to write about texts you've read, how to critically respond to texts you've read, and—of course—how to build all of this up into an essay, from the first sentence of the introduction to the last sentence of your conclusion. We also devote a module to advice on how to do well on essay exams.
	Because of this step-by-step approach, we have carefully designed these modules for you to work through in order.
Part 2: Grammar, Mechanics, and Style	Modules 1 through 8 in Part 2 support the topics in Part 1 by helping you develop key "mechanical" skills in terms of grammar, punctuation, style, and related topics.
	Unlike the modules in Part 1, you do not necessarily need to read these modules in order. Your teacher may work through these modules in order, or not. In any case, you should definitely read 2.1 and 2.2 before reading the others because these two modules introduce some basic principles that all the other modules use. Aside from these opening modules, you can dip into Part 2 as needed, based on what your teacher is doing in class, based on your own questions about the topics, or both.
	You can read more about how Part 1 and Part 2 fit together in Module 1.1, which gives you a detailed roadmap for the book.

Acknowledgements

The authors wish to acknowledge everyone who helped make this book a reality.

In particular, we would like to thank our friends and family, who provided encouragement throughout the writing and revision process: Doug, Anita, and Dana Feltham; Craig and Yvonne Meahan; Selma Purac; and Kate Kennedy. We'd also like to thank the good people at the Tea Haus at Covent Garden Market in London, Ontario, for timely infusions of caffeine.

We would like to thank the many reviewers whose comments and suggestions helped to improve the final version of the book.

Last, but certainly not least, we are very grateful to our editors at Oxford University Press, without whom this book would not exist. We especially thank Jeff Gulley for helping get the project off the ground, Jason Tomassini for his consistent encouragement and skilful management of administrative and contractual details, Cindy Angelini for her editing and guidance during the early phases of the book's composition, and Leslie Saffrey for her excellent copyediting of the final manuscript. Most importantly, we are deeply grateful to Carolyn Pisani for her tireless editorial efforts to make this book what it is today.

Mark Feltham, Wm. Paul Meahan, and Whitney Hoth

REVIEWERS

Oxford University Press Canada would like to express appreciation to the instructors and coordinators who graciously offered feedback on *Writing Critically* at various stages of the developmental process. Their feedback was instrumental in helping to shape and refine the series.

Jason Bourget
Martha Burnett
Calum Cunningham
Brian Dunphy
Melissa Dunphy
Jamie Johnston
Haytham Mahfoud

Jeff Miles
Julie P. Morris
Robert Muhlbock
Geoffrey Ruelland
Stephanie Samboo
Jaclyn Smith-Wilson
Trisha Yeo

Author Team

A native of St. John's, Newfoundland, **Mark Feltham** received his PhD in English from the University of Western Ontario in 2004. He has taught at both Western (2001–2005) and Fanshawe College (2005–present). In addition to teaching mostly writing and professional communication courses, he also has research interests in both higher-education policy and writing pedagogy, especially regarding the role of grammar in writing teaching, the writing needs of nurses, and approaches to teaching revision.

Wm. Paul Meahan received his MA in English from the University of Western Ontario in 2002. After working as a teaching assistant at Western and the University of Toronto, he joined the School of Language and Liberal Studies at Fanshawe College in 2007. In addition to teaching writing and professional communications, Paul has worked extensively to develop breadth curriculum at both the diploma and applied-degree levels. He has recently served as the Coordinator for both the General Education and Communications curricula at Fanshawe. He is a native of London, Ontario.

Whitney Hoth has taught at colleges and universities in both the United States and Canada, including the University of Michigan, Fort Hays State University in Kansas, Del Mar College and Laredo Community College in Texas, and Ryerson University, University of Waterloo, and Fanshawe College in Ontario. He served as Chair of the School of Language and Liberal Studies at Fanshawe College from 2005 to 2011. He is the author, together with Dr. Roger Fisher, of a comprehensive study of Ontario College communications teaching practices, *College-Level Literacy* (2010), sponsored by the Higher Education Quality Council of Ontario (HEQCO). Working with his colleagues Juan Flores, and Drs. Cheryl Pfoff and Mark Feltham, he has helped develop and implement several college-level writing programs reflecting principles and strategies deriving from the foundational work of Mina P. Shaughnessy (1924–1978).

Critical Reading and Critical Response

Student Roadmap for This Book

Yes, You *Can* Write

Organization: The Book

Organization: The Modules

Your First Assignment

"Students Need a Gap Year"

"The Future = Math Required"

[MODULE **1.1**]

Student Roadmap for This Book

Yes, You *Can* Write

Writing well—*really* well—can take years of practice. However, if you're reading this book, you don't have years to spare: you need to develop your writing skills immediately, most likely because you're in a college or university program.

How often have you heard someone declare, "I can't write"? Have you ever said it yourself? We hate to disagree on the very first page, but the fact is that you *can* write. You have been developing your writing and reading skills since you were very young, and in reading these words, you're applying advanced language skills that took years to develop. Imagine trying to read these words in a language that you don't know, and you'll understand what we mean. Yes, some people are better readers and writers than others, and natural ability probably plays a role, but everyone can improve as a writer. This book is all about how.

We can't promise this book will make you an expert writer overnight, or even over the course of one semester, but there are specific things you can do now that will noticeably improve your writing fairly quickly. We make this prediction based on our 40-plus years of experience improving our own writing and helping college and university students improve theirs.

Organization: The Book

This book has two parts, and each part has separate modules. References to modules within the book combine both the part number and the module number, like this: 1.1 means Part 1, Module 1.

The modules in Part 1 are designed for you to work through in order: this part covers key essay-writing skills. If you glance at the table of contents or skim through the modules, however, you'll notice that we don't get into the usual details of essay writing until Module 1.5. Why?

Modules 1.2 through 1.4 are all about some key reading and thinking skills that get you ready to write. Writing usually has to be *about* something, and college and university writing is usually about responding to assigned readings of various sorts. We start there.

Part 2 is about grammar, sentence structure, punctuation, and other related topics. Although the modules in Part 2 follow a logical order, they are not designed to be read in order after the modules in Part 1. Instead, your teacher will likely work through Part 2 modules in combination with Part 1 modules. We recommend that you read Modules 2.1 and 2.2 as soon as possible. Your teacher may give you more detailed information about how to combine Part 2 with Part 1.

Organization: The Modules

Except for this introductory module, each module in this book follows the same pattern, and recognizing this pattern will help you understand the contents.

Objectives and Self-Checks

Beginning in 1.2, each module opens with objectives that tell you what you will learn in that module. These objectives will be very useful headers for your notes. Next comes a self-check activity. You'll probably already know some of the terms and ideas in the objectives. Some of the information will be a review of basic principles, but much will be new. The self-check activity helps you determine what you already know and what you may need to add to your knowledge. You will find another self-check near the end. This second self-check will help you to remember the most important concepts covered in each module. We strongly recommend that you take the time to complete these self-checks, as doing so will help you see how your skills are developing.

The Main Event

After the objectives and the first self-check, you will usually find a question or short activity. Don't worry if you don't know the answers to these opening questions: you will by the end of the module. The point is to get you thinking about what follows. Next comes the main section of the module, which presents the explanations, examples, and tips that help you improve your writing.

You should spend most of your time working through this material and doing the activities that come at the end.

Wrapping Things Up

Before these activities, you will find a module checklist and a short section called "Looking Ahead." This checklist is especially important because it presents key concepts as brief, practical statements you can apply to your writing. "Looking Ahead" does exactly what the name suggests: it explains how each module relates to what comes next, both short term and long term.

Module Activities

The activities are an important part of the module because they test your ability to understand and apply concepts. Some activities involve single sentences, but many include recognizing, identifying, and correcting a range of errors requiring writing and rewriting. We also include several activities that involve exchanging and comparing results with a partner or a group. Some activities, especially in Part 2, require that you go over things you have written and assess and correct your own work. We believe these activities will give you an opportunity to see how questions about writing often have more than one correct answer, and it is valuable to see how other classmates respond to the situations these activities present. Students can learn just as much from each other as they can from this book and from their teachers.

Your teacher may not ask you to complete all the activities for each module; he or she may add additional activities. In either case, we recommend writing out your answers to the activities. You may decide to write the answers in your book, but for some activities, you may need to use a separate piece of paper or perhaps your computer. In most cases, *how* you do them is less important than going through the process and working with the concepts.

Some of these activities have clear answers, but others are more open-ended and encourage you to experiment with different approaches to solving writing problems. When in doubt, ask your teacher for advice and feedback on your approaches to the activities.

Your First Assignment

As we said earlier, writing in college, university, and the workplace tends to involve responding to something the writer has read. To illustrate the writing principles necessary in such situations, many of the examples in this book focus on two short essays, each of which you will find below. Your teacher also has access to many more essays and may add additional readings to your classes.

To get started, please read the following two essays.

STUDENTS NEED A GAP YEAR

by Louise Zacarias

1   Eighteen-year-olds are too immature to start college and university right after high school. Eighteen-year-olds are basically children. Their immaturity has several elements. For example, they lack proper time-management skills, they haven't lived on their own before, and they aren't used to taking responsibility for their own actions. These characteristics stop post-secondary students from succeeding. To solve this problem, colleges and universities should not admit students directly after high school. Instead, they should require that students take a "gap year" before signing up for more school.

2   The term "gap year" became well known in North America back in 2000 when Prince William took time off between high school and university to do volunteer work. However, students don't need to be royalty to benefit from some time off from school before starting post-secondary education. All students can benefit from such time off, time to work, time to volunteer, and, most importantly, time to become generally more mature before confronting the demands of college and university, which require that students be much more independent than they are in high school.

3   When students start college or university, they often experience quite a jolt: they go from high school graduation through a few months of a summer job straight into a very different educational environment. In high school, they lived at home, and their parents took care of a lot of responsibilities that students suddenly have to take on themselves when they go away to college or university—responsibilities that add stress at the same time as students encounter even more new stress associated with the increased demands of post-secondary education. These new stresses, which all begin in the September following high school graduation, make it much harder for students to be successful during their post-secondary studies. Currently, more than 50 per cent of all incoming first-year students to Canadian universities are seriously unprepared to manage the stress levels they encounter.

If students experienced a "gap year" between the end of high school and the start   4
of post-secondary education, they would not encounter all these new stresses
at the same time. Instead, they would have more time to adapt to these new
responsibilities and life circumstances, and they would also have a year of extra
maturity when they finally start school again. Certainly students can take a year
off now if they want to do so, but letting them have the choice isn't enough.
What if they make the wrong choice, and start post-secondary education when
they aren't yet ready? If they fail out or underperform because of a lack of maturity and the stresses of increased responsibilities, no one benefits.

For these reasons, to make sure that all students are sufficiently mature and   5
ready to meet the challenges of post-secondary education, colleges and universities should all require that students take at least a year off between the end of
high school and the start of any additional schooling.

THE FUTURE = MATH REQUIRED

by Mae Agnesi

1   We hear a great deal these days about illiteracy—a disturbing percentage of the population cannot read and write well enough, people keep saying, to succeed in our current economy, where a well-developed mind makes more money than well-developed muscles. As an English teacher, I certainly agree. However, despite the fact that I'm an English teacher, I'm also a "math sympathizer": perhaps it's because I started my university studies in science, but I am routinely horrified by the lack of mathematical awareness all around me. If the future needs people who can read and write well, it also definitely needs people who can handle numbers, and it seems like many students are being horribly left behind. To fix this problem, we should require that all college students—regardless of their program—take math courses.

2   Students cannot calculate basic percentages. Students cannot figure out change when they buy something, possibly because they are so used to Interac doing it for them. Students do not understand statistics, and our world runs on statistics: statistics inform most business and public-policy decisions in advanced societies such as the one we live in. When students can deal with numbers, they usually need calculators to do so, and they often do not understand the numbers going in or coming out.

3   Here is an example. I witnessed this problem recently when a student of mine needed to use a calculator to turn ¾ into a percentage. He must have entered the numbers wrong, because his calculator told him that ¾ equals 50 per cent. Now, 3 is clearly more than half of 4, so ¾ cannot possibly be 50 per cent. And yet, the student said, out loud, "Wow, I only got 50 per cent!" The amazing thing is that he thought he had actually gotten 50 per cent. Of course, his actual mark was 75 per cent, but the fact that he didn't realize this fact is a horrifying criticism of our education system.

4   In other words, when students need a calculator to convert ¾ to a percentage, and when they don't realize they have gotten it wrong, we definitely have a

problem. Clearly the solution is more math courses. Students do not seem to be getting the math they need in high school, so we need to add more math courses to college programs. After all, there are few careers that don't involve math in some way: engineers and computer specialists are obvious examples, but nurses need to know drug dosages, and even people who work in retail or food-service jobs need to do some math, even with computers and cash registers to help them out.

To avoid graduating a generation of innumerates, we need more math, and we   5
need it immediately.

Breaking Down Arguments

What's Your Point?

Main and Supporting Points

[MODULE **1.2**]

Breaking Down Arguments

Module Objectives

Upon successful completion of this module, you will be able to

1. define the terms *main point/thesis* and *supporting point*
2. recognize certain key words that indicate relationships between main and supporting points (for example, *because, thus, therefore, so*)
3. recognize the main parts of an argument
4. distinguish between main and supporting points in texts of varying lengths

---

Self-Check **1**

Read the module objectives above. You've probably encountered some of these terms and concepts before; others, however, will likely be new. In point form, identify what seems familiar and what seems new to you in the chart below.

What do I already know about the topics in this module's objectives?	What seems new to me?

What's Your Point?

You have probably heard this common phrase: "What's your point?" When people ask this question, they are usually asking for someone to state a claim or position.

In argumentative writing, the most important—or main—point is usually called a thesis statement, or thesis for short. It is very important to remember that when people make statements, or points, they make them for a reason. Sometimes people specifically give the reason, as in this example:

> We should move to a new apartment because our neighbours are too noisy.

Sometimes the reasons are implied, such as when someone says,

> Let's order a pizza.

Usually there is no need to say "Let's order a pizza because I'm hungry." In this example, the reason is clear without saying it. In other cases, however, the reasons are not clear. In the example below, the reasons behind the statement gradually emerge during a conversation:

> We should start going to the supermarket downtown.

If someone made this statement without giving a reason, you would probably want to know why. Certainly a variety of reasons are possible, as becomes clear here:

> We should start going to the supermarket downtown.

> Why?

> It's cheaper.

> It is for some things, sure, but it's also a lot further away than the other one. We'll have to spend more on gas to drive there, and besides, it's always too crowded.

> Oh, we won't really spend that much more on gas, and it's not crowded in the mornings when we usually shop anyway.

Notice the logical structure here, which you could write out like this:

> We should start going to the supermarket downtown **because** it's cheaper.

Although it's cheaper for some things, it's a lot further away, **so** we'll have to spend more on gas to drive there. **Also**, it's too crowded.

We will spend a little more on gas; **however**, it won't be very much more. **Also**, it isn't crowded in the mornings. **Because** we shop in the mornings, the crowds won't bother us then.

Writing a conversation out in such detail seems strange: people don't usually talk this way. In casual conversation, we don't always spell everything out in full logical detail. Unlike conversation, formal writing tends to use more words that reveal how ideas are connected.

Speakers often rely on context and non-verbal cues to communicate meaning and understanding. Writers, however, are forced to use more exact language to ensure logical relations and connections are clear.

In a conversation, after all, the context is usually clear because the people are often in the same place, and if there is any confusion, they can ask for clarification. In writing, though, the writer is almost never around when the reader is reading, so writing has to be perfectly clear from the beginning. This need for extra clarity is why writing has to spell so much out. If you have ever had a miscommunication in an exchange involving email or texting, you understand the importance of exact language.

Go back to the supermarket passage above and look at the coloured words. These words indicate the relationships between statements: they provide connections between ideas, and they often indicate when the speaker is providing a *reason* for the proposed action or idea.

There are many connection words, but the most common ones are summarized in the following chart.

Causes/Reasons/Results	Examples
as a result because since so therefore thus	My alarm clock didn't go off this morning; **as a result**, I was late.
	Because my alarm clock didn't go off this morning, I was late.
	My alarm clock didn't go off this morning, **so** I was late.

Contrast	Examples
although but however nevertheless while	**Although** I have no children, my sister has one son. I have no children, **but** my sister has one son. I have no children; **however**, my sister has one son.
Sequence	**Examples**
also and furthermore in addition/additionally moreover	Late on Saturday morning I went for coffee, **and** I met a friend for lunch right afterward. Late on Saturday morning I went for coffee; **also**, I met a friend for lunch right afterward. Late on Saturday morning I went for coffee; **in addition**, I met a friend for lunch right afterward.

The same sentence can combine different connection words:

Although it's cheaper for some things, it's a lot further away, so we'll have to spend more on gas to drive there.

Although combines with *so* to indicate both a contrast and a reason. Be careful, though, not to overload your sentences with too many connection words, or your writing may become confusing.

When you propose to do something (such as going to a different supermarket) and then provide *reasons* for doing so, you are making an argument. When people hear the word *argument*, they sometimes think of people yelling at each other while having some sort of angry disagreement. Although people do often use the word *argument* to mean conflict, we are using the word with a more specific meaning: in this book, **argument** refers to a set of statements linked logically and backed up with reasons. Usually, there is a central statement, or main point, that suggests that we should perform (or stop performing) some action. Sometimes the argument is not specifically about an action. Instead, the main point could also be that the reader should change the way that he or she thinks about an issue.

argument
An argument refers to a set of statements linked logically and backed up with reasons.

In the example on page 15, the speaker's main point is that the couple should start going to a new supermarket. It is easy to identify the main point in this example, and identifying a main point is always the first step in making and analyzing an argument, but having a main point alone is never enough to make a good argument. Any person presenting an argument also needs to give reasons for the main point: these reasons are called supporting points.

Main and Supporting Points

So now we have two kinds of points: main and supporting. We have already seen that when people ask "What's your point?" they are usually asking about the main point of an argument, and the main point is usually a statement about what someone should or should not do. But you have also heard people say "That's a good point." The term *point* here usually refers to a specific *part* of an argument or debate: it might be a fact, a statistic, or an example that supports the main point. As you will see, not all points are the same. In order to understand arguments and write your own, you need to understand this important difference between main and supporting points.

The sentences in the following paragraph present a series of points:

> We should ask the teacher for a one-week extension on our essay because he was late giving us the topic. Because of this delay, we didn't have as much time to work on it as we needed. Also, he was sick for several days, so we are behind schedule. He might give us a full extra week; however, he might only give us an extra few days. If we don't ask, we won't get anything, so we should ask right away.

If you break this paragraph down into points, you get something like this:

1. We should ask the teacher for a one-week extension on our essay.
2. He was late giving us the topic.
3. We didn't have as much time to work on it as we needed.
4. He was sick for several days.
5. We are behind schedule.
6. He might give us a full extra week.
7. He might only give us an extra few days.
8. We don't ask.
9. We won't get anything.
10. We should ask right away.

These points are not all equally important. The most important point, the point on which all the others depend, is the point in the first part of the first sentence, point number 1: "We should ask the teacher for a one-week extension on our essay." This point is called the **main point**, and it appears again, for emphasis, in the last sentence. As we saw earlier in the module, this "main point" is basically the **thesis** of this particular paragraph: the overall argument that the students are trying to make here is that they should get an extension on their assignment.

Without this main point, all the other points would add up to nothing. They would be random reasons lacking a statement to support. Similarly, without supporting points, this main point would just be a statement without reasons. Main points and supporting points always work together to create an argument, and distinguishing between main and supporting points is an important first step in understanding and making arguments.

The next four points after the main point are all reasons given to justify, back up, or support the main point that the teacher should give us more time. Points 2, 3, 4, and 5 are **supporting points**.

Although the example above begins with the main point and then provides the supporting points, a different order is possible:

> The teacher was late giving us the topic for our essay. Because of this delay, we didn't have as much time to work on it as we needed. Also, he was sick for several days, so we are behind schedule. Therefore, we should ask the teacher for a one-week extension on our essay. He might give us a full extra week; however, he might only give us an extra few days. If we don't ask, we won't get anything, so we should ask right away.

One good way to recognize main points is to think about what the writer or speaker recommends in terms of an action: something someone should or should not do. Position (in the sentence or paragraph) alone isn't enough to tell you if a point is main or supporting.

Even simple statements can go both ways:

> Because the car repairs were very expensive, we couldn't afford to go on vacation this year.

> We couldn't afford to go on vacation this year because the car repairs were very expensive.

---

main point
In an argument, the main point is what the writer would like the reader to do or not do or think or not think.

thesis
The term *thesis* is very closely related to the term *main point*. In general, a writer's thesis is a statement regarding the writer's main point.

supporting point
A supporting point is a reason given to back up the main point.

The car repairs were very expensive; therefore, we couldn't afford to go on vacation this year.

The car repairs were very expensive, so we couldn't afford to go on vacation this year.

No matter how you write these sentences, the basic idea is the same: the expensive car repairs are the reason (supporting point) for not being able to afford a vacation (main point).

Although many situations are more complicated than these examples, you can usually figure out the main and supporting points of an argument by asking the following questions:

Question	Answer	Example
What should we do or not do (or think or not think)?	answer = **main point**	We should start going to the supermarket downtown.
Why should we do it or not do it (or think or not think it)?	answer = **supporting point** (a reason for the main point)	The prices are lower there.

Understanding how points connect is the key to understanding arguments.

Module Checklist

Can I

☐ define the terms *main point* and *supporting point*?

☐ recognize the difference between main and supporting points in an argument?

☐ recognize a thesis statement in a piece of writing?

☐ break down a sustained argument into its component parts?

☐ recognize transitional words that link together main and supporting points?

Looking Ahead

You have to understand an argument before you can respond to it. To write a response to someone else's work, you need to know clearly what that person is trying to convince you to do or think, so being able to identify a writer's thesis is crucial to the task of writing a critical response.

In the next two modules, you will encounter sample texts each containing a main point (the thesis) and also the many supporting points used to justify this thesis. These supporting points are the writer's evidence for his or her primary claims, and as you will see, they can range from strong to weak points. We will look at how to identify and summarize source texts and how to think about them critically.

Recognizing main and supporting points is a skill you can apply in many ways. In other courses, if you can distinguish the main point in each textbook chapter, you'll have a better idea about what to focus on for tests and exams. If you can quickly determine the main point in an email from your boss, you'll be able to jump right in to the task that you've been assigned. If you can identify the supporting points in an argument with which you disagree, you can point out logical flaws and provide reasoned resistance. When you learn to break down an argument, you also learn how to prioritize information, and that skill can help you in many different writing situations, such as research papers, proposals, technical reports, and marketing plans.

Self-Check 2

Refer back to the first self-check at the beginning of this module. Have your ideas changed? What new ideas do you have? Write them out in the chart below.

Based on the objectives at the start, how have my views changed since the beginning of this module?	What new information do I have?

Activities

Before turning to the next module, check your understanding of the concepts and terms of this module by completing the activities below.

1. In each sentence below, circle the main point and underline the supporting point.

   a) Let's wait until after the holidays to buy our new TV. Everything will be on sale then.

   b) My alarm clock didn't go off, so I was late this morning. Please don't fire me.

   c) Because of the immense popularity of *Avatar*, movie studios started making many more 3D movies to expand their market.

   d) The Toronto Blue Jays spend much less than the Yankees or Red Sox on player salaries; therefore, the Jays will need to increase payroll significantly to compete.

   e) I'd rather buy a new iPhone before an iPad, to be honest, but I just got a new cell phone, so getting another new phone right away would be a waste. I'm thus going to buy an iPad first, then an iPhone in about a year.

2. Read the following introductory paragraph from Louise Zacarias' "Students Need a Gap Year" (found on page 8), and complete the activities that follow:

   Eighteen-year-olds are too immature to start college and university right after high school. Eighteen-year-olds are basically children. Their immaturity has several elements. For example, they lack proper time-management skills, they haven't lived on their own before, and they aren't used to taking responsibility for their own actions. These characteristics stop post-secondary students from succeeding. To solve this problem, colleges and universities should not admit students directly after high school. Instead, they should require that students take a "gap year" before signing up for more school.

   a) Louise Zacarias' introduction has been rewritten below to demonstrate how key connecting words draw attention to the relationship between main and supporting points. Fill in the blanks using connecting words

from the table in the section "What's Your Point?" on pages 16 and 17.
You may repeat words, provided that they fit the context.

> Eighteen-year-olds are basically children, _____
> they are too immature to start college or university right after
> high school. Young post-secondary students frequently struggle at
> college/university _____ they aren't used to taking
> responsibility for their own actions. _____ they lack
> time-management skills and haven't lived on their own before,
> recent high-school graduates won't succeed in college or university.
> _____ these struggles are a common problem, colleges
> and universities should require students to wait a year for admission.
> A "gap year" will require students to gain maturity before beginning
> post-secondary studies; _____, the students will be
> more successful in the long run.

b) On a separate sheet of paper, summarize Zacarias' main point/thesis
   using your own words. Give two reasons why Zacarias believes what
   she does, using a different "Causes/Reasons/Results" word (from
   the same table in the "What's Your Point?" section on page 16) for
   each sentence. Then, write one sentence that disagrees with Zacarias'
   overall argument using one (or more) of the "Contrast" words from
   the same table.

3. Read the following introductory paragraph from Mae Agnesi's
   "The Future = Math Required" (found on page 10), and complete the
   activities that follow:

> We hear a great deal these days about illiteracy—a disturbing
> percentage of the population cannot read and write well enough,
> people keep saying, to succeed in our current economy, where a well-
> developed mind makes more money than well-developed muscles. As
> an English teacher, I certainly agree. However, despite the fact that
> I'm an English teacher, I'm also a "math sympathizer": perhaps it's
> because I started my university studies in science, but I am routinely
> horrified by the lack of mathematical awareness all around me. If the
> future needs people who can read and write well, it also definitely needs
> people who can handle numbers, and it seems like many students are
> being horribly left behind. To fix this problem, we should require that
> all college students—regardless of their program—take math courses.

In pairs, and on a separate sheet of paper or on your computer, follow these steps:

a) In your own words, write out Agnesi's main point/thesis. Explain, in point form, why Agnesi believes her idea is the right solution to this problem.

b) Consider one objection to Agnesi's claims. What are the potential problems with her proposed solution?

c) Copy the formula below, and fill in the blanks with the ideas you've written down in response to (a) and (b):

Agnesi believes _____ because
[main point/thesis]

_____ .
[one supporting point]

Additionally, Agnesi thinks that _____ .
[second supporting point]

However, Agnesi fails to consider _____ .
[one main point that contradicts her claims]

Thus, her idea cannot be supported.

4. The following passage is a short proposal to an employer. Read through the passage, then follow the instructions below it.

A Proposal: Mandatory Fitness Classes for Employees

by Nick Adamley

Research has shown that regular exercise provides numerous physical and mental benefits, including better general health, lower blood pressure, lower cholesterol, and reduced stress levels. For these reasons, several companies have begun providing fitness classes to their employees. Companies have found that these classes have numerous benefits for the employer: employees who are healthier and less stressed are more productive, call in sick less often, and are generally better employees. Our company should make fitness classes a requirement for all employees: for a small amount of money to pay for these classes, our company can obtain numerous benefits.

As you know, there is a private gym just down the street from our offices. This gym has several personal trainers on staff, and they could easily conduct classes for our employees at various times per week. Our employees could travel there quite easily, or their trainers could come here, if our employees do not have time to leave the office.

I know from talking to many of the employees in our office that they already go to the gym, so they would welcome the opportunity to have fitness classes during work hours, especially if the company paid for them.

To get the greatest benefit for all employees, the company should make these fitness classes a requirement: if everyone has to participate, then the benefits to the company of increased employee health will be as great as possible.

Now consult the table with the three types of connectors on pages 16–17. Based on Adamley's proposal, complete the following tasks, either on a separate sheet of paper or on your computer.

a) Summarize Adamley's ideas in your own words by filling in the blanks in the following formula. Link the points with an appropriate connector.

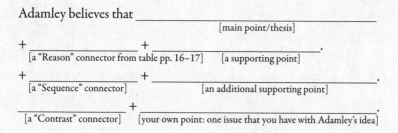

Adamley believes that _____
                                        [main point/thesis]
+ _____ + _____.
  [a "Reason" connector from table pp. 16–17]   [a supporting point]
+ _____ + _____.
  [a "Sequence" connector]   [an additional supporting point]

_____ + _____.
[a "Contrast" connector]   [your own point: one issue that you have with Adamley's idea]

Your answer should look something like this:

Mae Agnesi believes that students should be required to take postsecondary math courses
[main point/thesis]

because
[a "Reason" connector]

they will be "left behind" in future jobs that require math skills.
[a supporting point]

In addition,
[a "Sequence" connector]

she points out the importance of understanding how statistics work "in advanced societies such as the one we live in."
[an additional supporting point]

However,
[a "Contrast" connector]

Agnesi's argument assumes that all students are the same even though many students have excellent math skills.
[your own point: one issue that you have with Agnesi's idea]

b) Compare your summary to that of a classmate. You probably didn't make exactly the same choices. Review each other's work. What might account for some of the differences in your two responses?

c) Working together with your partner, rewrite your paragraph, selecting the best words and phrases from each version.

d) Using chalkboards, whiteboards, or flip-chart paper (depending on what's in your classroom and what your teacher would like you to do), write out your summary from (c) and compare your work with that of your classmates.

5. For more practice, ask your teacher for another argumentative essay. Read it and then complete Activities 4(a) through (d) for that new text. Of course, you'll have to change the name *Adamley* in 4(a) to the name of the author of the new essay.

6. Pick a text from outside this course. Choose a magazine article, a newspaper article, or a section of a textbook for another course.

a) Identify the main and supporting points of the text you selected.

b) Write down any "Reason," "Sequence," or "Contrast" words you see the author using to relate the main points to the supporting points.

c) For each word you have identified in (b) above, write down a word that would have the same meaning and accomplish the same goal.

Referring to Texts

[MODULE 1.3]

Referring to Texts

Module Objectives

Upon successful completion of this module, you will be able to

1. explain why writers need to refer to texts
2. use signal phrases with correct punctuation and appropriate verbs to integrate quotations, paraphrases, and summaries within the structure of larger sentences
3. vary signal phrases
4. define the terms *direct quotation*, *paraphrase*, and *summary*
5. explain the benefits and drawbacks of direct quotation, paraphrase, and summary
6. explain the importance of quotation marks
7. use correct conventions for referring to authors in signal phrases
8. sequence direct quotations, summaries, and paraphrases to explain the basic argumentative structure of a short text

Self-Check 1

Read the module objectives above. You've probably encountered some of these terms and concepts before; others, however, will likely be new. In point form, identify what seems familiar and what seems new to you in the chart below.

What do I already know about the topics in this module's objectives?	What seems new to me?

So Then She Said . . .

Consider the following groups of words. What do they have in common?

As my brother always points out, . . .

My dad called to tell me that . . .

The synopsis to Section 75 of
Martin's Criminal Code of Canada
makes this point: . . .

So then he says . . .

She texted me
back that . . .

In his study of Berlin during
World War II, Roger Moorhouse
argues that . . .

He wrote me back
and said that . . .

I said that . . .

On page 22, the company
policy manual states . . .

My boss emailed
me to say . . .

Although these expressions are quite different, they all do the same thing: they all refer to information from somewhere else.

For example, you might be telling a friend about your Friday night, you might be describing a text message, you might be writing a research paper, or you might be training a new hire at work.

All the phrases in the figure above are examples of **signal phrases**. The word *signal* might make you think of signals on a car, which show other drivers where you are *going*. However, when you use a signal phrase in writing, you are indicating where an idea has *come from*.

These phrases are extremely important because they help writers and readers keep track of the words and ideas of others. These phrases reveal the sources of whatever comes next: a quotation, paraphrase, or summary. Without signal phrases, a reader may be confused about the source of a word or phrase.

signal phrase
A signal phrase signals to the reader that what follows is written or verbal information from somewhere else.

Signal phrases are everywhere: in letters, emails, newspaper and magazine stories (either online or not), reports, text messages, and yes, essays. In this module, we focus mainly on their use in essays, but you should keep in mind that signal phrases occur in other types of writing as well, and they generally work the same way in any kind of text.

Types of Signal Phrases

Look back at the examples above. There are three features to note:

- They all specify who said (or wrote) the information.
- They all have verbs (*said*, *texted*, *wrote*, and so on) that describe how the information was presented.
- Some of them have particular punctuation marks attached to them, while others have no punctuation.

Here are four common types of signal phrases used in writing:

1. _____ states that _____.
2. According to _____, _____.
3. As _____ states, _____.
4. _____ makes this point: _____.

Many different versions are possible, as you'll learn later.

Notice the differences in punctuation: the first one has no punctuation after the signal phrase, while signal phrases 2 and 3 use commas. In contrast, signal phrase 4 uses a colon.

Three of the four have verbs in the signal phrase itself; signal phrase 2 would have the verb in the second part, represented by the second blank after the comma.

How to Use Signal Phrases: The Basics

In an essay, when you refer to another text, you usually need to identify or explain your reference so your reader will understand it. You should *not* assume your reader has read the text to which you're referring. You need to identify the original text and *explain* its significance in a clear and organized way.

Whether or not your reader already knows the text or source under discussion in your essay, summarizing and explaining it in a clear and organized way allows the reader to understand why you are referring to it and what function it serves in your argument. In other words, as another writing textbook entitled *They Say/I Say* suggests, you have to explain what the original author says *before* you can add his or her words and thoughts to your own argument.

Here are some examples of signal phrases used to introduce readers to arguments in "The Future = Math Required," written by Mae Agnesi (see page 10).

1. In "The Future = Math Required," Mae Agnesi states that we require "people who can handle numbers, and it seems like many students are being horribly left behind," so "we should require that all college students—regardless of their program—take math courses."

2. In "The Future = Math Required," Mae Agnesi argues that because students lack the math skills needed for their future careers, colleges should make math courses mandatory for all college students.

3. In "The Future = Math Required," Mae Agnesi argues that colleges should make math courses mandatory for all college students.

A glance at the above sentences will reveal both similarities and differences among these three sentences:

Similar	Different
Each sentence starts by giving the title in quotation marks and the author's full name (first name and last name, exactly as provided).	In (1) the writer uses Agnesi's exact words: notice the quotation marks around these words, which express Agnesi's main point/thesis and one of her supporting points.
Each sentence uses the same signal phrase pattern: "states that" or "argues that" without any punctuation after the word *that*.	In (2), the writer gives the same points as in (1), but in his or her own words.
Each sentence has the verb in the present tense. Unless you're using a system that requires otherwise, use the present tense when referring to a source text.	In (3), the writer gives only Agnesi's main point, but in his or her own words.

Some systems for referring to texts require past-tense verbs in certain situations. You will learn more about such systems when you learn about writing full research essays.

e on page 31 illustrates a different technique for present-
source:

(sometimes called "direct quotation")

2. paraphrase

3. summary

The next section provides more information about each technique.

Quotation, Paraphrase, and Summary

Technique	Basic definition	Example	Original text
Quotation	Integrate the exact words of the source text into your own sentence, using quotation marks. Note: Borrowed language absolutely requires quotation marks in most cases (longer quotations are sometimes formatted as blocks without quotation marks, but this will be covered later).	In "The Future = Math Required," Mae Agnesi states that we require "people who can handle numbers, and it seems like many students are being horribly left behind," so "we should require that all college students—regardless of their program—take math courses."	"If the future needs people who can read and write well, it also definitely needs people who can handle numbers, and it seems like many students are being horribly left behind. To fix this problem, we should require that all college students— regardless of their program— take math courses."
Paraphrase	Present roughly the same details as appear in a passage from a source text, but in your own words.	In "The Future = Math Required," Mae Agnesi argues that because students lack the math skills needed for their future careers, colleges should make math courses mandatory for all college students.	"If the future needs people who can read and write well, it also definitely needs people who can handle numbers, and it seems like many students are being horribly left behind. To fix this problem, we should require that all college students— regardless of their program— take math courses."
Summary	Present only the main point(s) of the source text, expressed in your own words.	In "The Future = Math Required," Mae Agnesi argues that colleges should make math courses mandatory for all college students.	"If the future needs people who can read and write well, it also definitely needs people who can handle numbers, and it seems like many students are being horribly left behind. To fix this problem, we should require that all college students— regardless of their program— take math courses."

When referring to a text, most writers combine all three of the techniques demonstrated in the examples above: direct quotation, paraphrase, and summary.

These three techniques have different advantages and disadvantages:

Technique	Advantages	Disadvantages
Quotation	There is no need to change the source text. Especially concise or distinctive passages from another writer can be borrowed to support your own writing. Exact words can be used as evidence to support your argument.	Excessive quotation can overpower your writing by giving too much space to the words of another writer. Integrating quotations requires special knowledge of sentence structure and punctuation (see Part 2 of this book).
Paraphrase	Paraphrase prevents over-quoting.	You must ensure a paraphrase is in your own words. Using the same words of a source text without quotation marks is plagiarism. Thus, paraphrasing takes longer than quoting.
Summary	References to a source can be compressed to leave space for your own responses and arguments.	Summaries can oversimplify a source text by leaving out too many important details.

plagiarism
Borrowing language from another source without quotation marks (or other formatting) is called plagiarism, a serious legal/academic offence that can result in zeros on assignments, failure in courses, and sometimes expulsion from college or university.

The next sections contain more information about each technique, along with discussions of some common problems.

Quotations and Quotation Integration

You must ensure that direct quotations from a source text are identical to the original wording and properly integrated into your own sentence, as in the following example:

> In "The Future = Math Required," Mae Agnesi states that we require "people who can handle numbers, and it seems like many students are being horribly left behind," so "we should require that all college students—regardless of their program—take math courses."

If you carefully read the words inside the quotation marks, you'll see the words are identical to those of the original. In addition, Agnesi's words fit neatly into the surrounding sentence without any awkwardness. This example uses the verb *require* to introduce the quotation ("people who can handle numbers").

Similarly, the example merges the second quotation from Agnesi into the new sentence by using the connecting word *so*. If you read the full sentence aloud from beginning to end, it all fits together.

quotation integration
A properly integrated quotation accurately reproduces the original text and fits neatly into your sentence.

The example on page 33 illustrates the principle of **quotation integration**: the original text is accurately reproduced and the words from the original fit seamlessly into the sentence. That's the key: the material inside must fit with the material outside.

Quotation integration can be tricky. You may need to tinker with the original quotation by cutting it with quotation marks at different places to make it fit. However, never cut words from the original in a way that changes its meaning! For instance, consider the following original quotation:

Colleges should not allow students to download media in residence.

Next, look closely at this cut-down version:

"Colleges should," according to some, "allow students to download media in residence."

This deletion is a form of deception because it eliminates a word from the original quotation in a way that actually changes the original quotation's meaning.

Paraphrase and Summary Must Be in Your Own Words

Paraphrase and summary differ in the level of detail they convey about a source; however, both must be in your own words. Rewriting a source in your own words can be difficult. Here is some advice to help you paraphrase and summarize properly.

Because rewriting everything in your own words takes a lot of time and effort, experienced writers usually use all three techniques: quotation, paraphrase, and summary. When writers draw on all three techniques, they can maximize their advantages while minimizing their disadvantages.

When you are putting ideas into your own words, make sure they are different words from the source. Also, don't simply plug in new words without changing the original word order: generally "your own words" means different words and different sentence structure as well.

Let's consider the following example:

> National Geographic's *Guide to the National Parks of Canada* notes that "Banff—the birthplace of the world's national park service—is part of UNESCO's Canadian Rocky Mountain World Heritage site. Located in the heart of the Canadian Rockies, the park boasts a cornucopia of postcard-perfect mountains."
>
> —Excerpt from National Geographic, *Guide to the National Parks of Canada*. Washington, D.C.: The National Geographic Society, 2011.

If all you do when you paraphrase is substitute certain words that generally mean the same thing, without changing the word order or sentence structure, you have committed plagiarism, as in this example:

> National Geographic describes Banff National Park as the origin of the Earth's national park organizations and a UNESCO Heritage location. It points out that Banff is situated in the core of the Canadian Rockies, where the park boasts a plethora of picturesque peaks.

This paraphrase is flawed in many ways. The writer has done little to change the original word and sentence order and has simply used a thesaurus—probably from his or her word processor—to plug in replacement words that mean the same thing. He or she has also occasionally used specific words from the original text. As a result, the paraphrase is unclear, awkwardly worded, and—above all—plagiarized.

However, we could legitimately paraphrase the original sentence:

> National Geographic describes Alberta's Banff National Park as a beautiful and historically important place. Not only was it Canada's first national park, but it also remains a scenic part of the Canadian Rockies to this day.

The purpose of paraphrase is to capture the essence of a source text in your own words, not to repeat the original's sentences using a word-for-word substitution in the same order. Here the writer has changed enough words to make it his or her own, but he or she has still reproduced the main ideas from the original source.

Paraphrasing and summarizing well requires practice. If you're not sure about a particular paraphrase or summary, ask your teacher for help, or, if possible, visit your school's writing centre—many colleges and universities have writing centres with writing tutors who help students with essays.

Varying Signal Phrases

As we learned above, signal phrases usually contain a verb that describes how the author presents his or her information:

> Agnesi **states** that "even people who work in retail or food-service jobs need to do some math, even with computers and cash registers to help them out."

The verb *states* works in this example because it accurately describes how Agnesi presents her information in her original essay: she provides general information to her readers about retail and food-service jobs.

In other cases, you might choose a different verb, as in this example:

> In "The Future = Math Required," Mae Agnesi **argues** that students "do not seem to be getting the math they need in high school, so we need to add more math courses to college programs."

Because this quotation is actually the main point of Agnesi's argument, you should use a more specific word than *states* here: *argues*. Remember, a statement of fact is not by itself an argument (though it can be a supporting point for an argument): in an argument, the writer (or speaker) usually asserts something debatable—something that you can agree or disagree with. If you are presenting a point a writer has made, and if it appears to be the writer's main point, it is generally better to use *argues* rather than *states*.

Of course, some statements are debatable. Imagine that you're moving, and you want a friend to help. Your friend doesn't want to help you on that day, so he says he's busy, but you happen to know that he's not. There are a few ways to deal with this situation.

If you were speaking to someone, you would probably indicate your disbelief by stressing the word *said*:

> Well, he *said* he was busy, but I know he isn't, so I guess he just doesn't want to help.

You can express this stress in writing with italics. You could also choose a different verb, like *claimed* (with or without italics for emphasis):

> Well, he claimed he was busy, but I know he isn't, so I guess he just doesn't want to help.

The point is, you should fit your verb to the material that you're quoting, summarizing, or paraphrasing.

Below is a list of verbs that fit different situations.

Situation	When you want to be completely factual/ neutral, use	When you want to emphasize an author's debatable/argumentative main point, use	When you are questioning what an author has written, use
Verbs	• states • declares • observes • notes • remarks • proposes	• argues • asserts • contends	• claims • opines (the verb which comes from the noun *opinion*) • believes • feels • justifies

The exception to the table above is the phrase "according to _____." This phrase does not have a verb. This phrase is relatively factual/neutral, but it can also suggest that the writer is mildly questioning the author while referring to his or her points.

Sequencing Your Points: Which Ones, in What Order?

As you can see, signal phrases both refer to an author's text and explain the text's points to the reader. Consider how you would begin to explain Mae Agnesi's main and supporting points to a reader who has *not* read the original article.

First, to establish context for your reader, begin by giving the title and the author and then immediately use a signal phrase to state the author's main point. You can use direct quotation, summary, paraphrase, or a mixture here, but be sure to follow the advice above for whatever you decide to do. Next, you should state and explain, again using signal phrases, the supporting points for this main point/thesis. Here you need to think back to Module 1.2: what are the supporting points for this thesis? Specifically, why does Agnesi think that math should be required?

Note that first you give the author's full name, and afterward use either the last name only or a pronoun (*he/she*). You should never use the author's first name only.

The following table illustrates what this explanation of Agnesi's main and supporting points might look like if you wrote it out using the advice from this module. The left-hand column presents signal phrases in example sentences as you might write them, while the right-hand column shows you *how* such a sentence helps you to explain Agnesi's article to *your* readers.

Explanation of Agnesi's argument	
What you should say	**Why you should say it**
1. In "The Future = Math Required," Mae Agnesi states that we require "people who can handle numbers, and it seems like many students are being horribly left behind," so "we should require that all college students—regardless of their program—take math courses."	1. This sentence provides the title of the essay, gives the author's full name, and uses a signal phrase to introduce the quotation giving Agnesi's main point/thesis.
2. As Agnesi states, she is "routinely horrified by the lack of mathematical awareness all around" her.	2. This sentence switches to the author's last name only and uses a quotation to begin a discussion of the author's supporting points. Note the integration that has taken place: the quotation has been cut to eliminate *am* and *me*, which no longer make sense. The writer has added *her* at the end to make the quotation fit into his or her sentence.
3. According to Agnesi, students have trouble with basic mathematical skills like calculating percentages and making change, and this trouble brings with it trouble with larger issues like understanding statistics.	3. This sentence changes to a new signal phrase and paraphrase, which follows the order of the points in Agnesi's essay.
4. Basically, she suggests that when people don't understand math, they don't understand the world.	4. This sentence switches to the pronoun *she* and continues paraphrasing the original.
5. Agnesi uses these points to justify her proposal that all students be required to take math at college.	5. This final sentence repeats the author's name and links the supporting points back to the main point by indicating their relationship to each other.

Students often wonder how long such an explanation of another text should be. For example, the left-hand column in the above table consists of five sentences that total 119 words. Much longer texts require much longer initial explanations. Also, keep in mind that this explanation would be followed by the rest of an essay about Agnesi's article, where more quotations, paraphrases, or summaries would be provided. (See Modules 1.5 to 1.8 for more information about the various parts of an essay.)

The Agnesi example above is certainly not the only way to explain the structure of a text—there are many different ways because there are many different writers. Until you have more experience, though, we suggest following the model that we present here. Also, your teacher may show you variations on this model.

Module Checklist

Have I

☐ introduced all references to a source (or sources) with signal phrases?

☐ punctuated my signal phrases correctly? (See the example signal phrases on page 30 to double-check the patterns.)

☐ placed quotation marks (or otherwise indicated a quotation with formatting) around borrowed language?

☐ carefully checked all of my summaries and paraphrases to make sure that they are entirely in my own words in order to avoid plagiarism?

☐ chosen appropriate signal-phrase verbs for the situation?

☐ written all signal-phrase verbs in the present tense (unless my teacher has specified otherwise)?

☐ varied my signal phrases?

☐ double-checked the wording of all of my direct quotations to ensure that they are accurate and integrated properly within my own sentences without changing the meaning of the original text?

☐ given the title of a source and the author's *full* name the first time I referred to it?

Looking Ahead

The skills you have learned in this module have two purposes. One short-term purpose is to prepare you for the next module on critical analysis. In Module 1.4, we discuss how to critically analyze a short argument in detail because we will later be completing full essays that critically respond to other texts like Agnesi's "The Future = Math Required."

A more important, long-term purpose of this module is to provide you with the skills you will need to respond to most forms of writing. Research papers require these skills, as most common systems for citing and documenting sources rely on signal phrases to introduce summaries, quotations, and paraphrases. Reports use these skills. Emails often use these skills. Studies, legal documents, memos, and business letters use these skills as well. Basically, most situations involving writing require these skills.

Self-Check 2

Refer back to the first self-check at the beginning of this module. Have your ideas changed? What new ideas do you have? Write them out in the chart below.

Based on the objectives at the start, how have my views changed since the beginning of this module?	What new information do I have?

Activities

Before turning to the next module, check your understanding of the concepts and terms of this module by completing the activities below.

1. a) An "elevator pitch" is an ultra-brief presentation about a particular topic—brief enough, in fact, to deliver on an elevator ride. Jot down some notes for an elevator pitch about the importance of the skills in this module. Imagine that the person hearing the pitch is currently unconvinced about why referring to texts clearly and correctly is important.

   b) With a partner, deliver your pitches to each other. Did you have material that your partner didn't? What did your pitch lack? Try combining your pitches into a single pitch that incorporates the best features of both.

2. On a separate sheet of paper, write out the following summary of the paragraph below, filling in the missing words and punctuation marks. Long blanks are for words and phrases; very short blanks are for punctuation marks.

   In _____ Louise Zacarias
   argues that _____ . As
   _____ ___ "eighteen-year-olds are
   basically children." _____
   her ____ they "lack proper time-management skills, they
   haven't lived on their own before, and they aren't used to
   taking responsibility for their own actions." She claims
   _____ "these characteristics
   stop post-secondary students from succeeding."

   Compare your answers with a classmate's, and check both your answers against the information in this module and your notes.

3. With a classmate (or by yourself, if you wish), rewrite the paragraph from Activity 2, making any necessary corrections.

4. Compare the following explanation of the content of "The Future = Math Required" to the one on page 38 in this module. What advice would you give the student who wrote it?

   According to Agnesi students can't do math. Mae says that they should have to take math. Students didn't learn math in high school.

Students can't do percentages, they can't make change, and they don't understand statistics, so they have problems because in the future math is required.

5. Rewrite the paragraph from Activity 4, making different choices: for example, vary the signal phrases, use paraphrases instead of direct quotations, and so on. You may also want to expand the paragraph.

6. a) Exchange your revised version with a partner. They are likely different. How? Are there aspects of one that are better than the other? Which ones and why? Combine your partner's version and your version into one, keeping the best features of both. Your teacher will give you more detailed instructions regarding this activity.

   b) Using a chalkboard, a whiteboard, or flip-chart paper (depending on what's in your classroom and what your teacher would like you to do), write out your final explanation of Agnesi's article and compare your work with that of all your classmates. Your teacher will give you more detailed instructions regarding this activity.

7. Your teacher will give you an essay. Read it, and then write a brief explanation of its argument. Follow the pattern given in the table on page 38 and the checklist on page 39.

Critical Response

[M O D U L E **1.4**]

Critical Response

Module Objectives

Upon successful completion of this module, you will be able to

1. define *critical thinking*, *critical analysis*, and *critical response*
2. explain the importance of critical response in academic situations
3. explain the importance of evidence in argumentation
4. identify some types of evidence needed to support argumentative statements
5. define the terms *evidentiary*, *practical*, and *ethical* within the context of critical analysis and response
6. make evidentiary, practical, and ethical critiques of arguments

Self-Check 1

Read the module objectives above. You've probably encountered some of these terms and concepts before; others, however, will likely be new. In point form, identify what seems familiar and what seems new to you in the chart below.

What do I already know about the topics in this module's objectives?	What seems new to me?

It's One or the Other—*Really*?

In "The Tangerine Factor," the last episode of Season 1 of the popular television comedy *The Big Bang Theory*, Penny, one of the main characters, has just broken up with her boyfriend. She's naturally upset and is complaining to Leonard, another main character. Here's how their conversation goes:

> **Penny:** Tell me the truth. Am I just an idiot who picks giant losers?
>
> **Leonard:** Noooo.
>
> **Penny:** Okay, so I pick good guys, but turn them into losers?
>
> **Leonard:** Of course not!
>
> **Penny:** Well, it's got to be one or the other. Which is it?

Source: "The Tangerine Factor." *The Big Bang Theory*, 2008. Reproduced with permission of Warner Bros. Television.

We've probably all felt like Penny does from time to time. Because she's upset, she's picked only two explanations for her situation. Both explanations are insulting to her (and to her ex!), but are they the only two explanations possible?

Of course they're not—it's possible, for example, to explain the situation in many different ways: most obviously, perhaps they just weren't suited to each other. Penny deliberately restricts herself to only two negative explanations, probably because she is angry at both her ex-boyfriend and at herself.

The lesson here, aside from the fact that anger can make people unreasonable, is that picking only two options out of the many available is a bad way of making a point! In recognizing this problem, you're already engaging in critical thinking—the topic of this module.

Yes, Do Judge: What Does *Critical* Mean, Anyway?

We often say "don't judge," and this advice usually works well when applied to personal decisions and relationships. However, in our daily lives, we actually have to judge all the time. Consider some recent events in your life that have required you to make a judgment about something. You've probably recently judged

- whether or not you had enough money to pay for something
- whether or not a plan that you had made was likely to work
- whether or not you should follow someone's advice
- whether or not you liked a particular song, movie, or TV show

We constantly make judgments about the world around us. Many times our judgments are on a small scale, and can be done quickly—almost unthinkingly.

However, sometimes judgments require significantly more thought ahead of time. If engineers do not judge bridge designs properly, the bridges might fall down; if managers do not judge business plans properly, their companies might go broke; if doctors do not judge patients' symptoms correctly, the patients might die. In fact, when we make bad decisions, we often say that we "*misjudged* the situation."

We have already analyzed arguments in terms of their main and supporting points, and we have examined different techniques for referring to source material, but now we need to examine critical thinking. What are we doing when we engage in *critical thinking*, *critical analysis*, and *critical response*? These are common terms that people hear all the time, but what do they really mean?

First, let's talk about the common element in all the terms—*critical*. The word *critical* is sometimes associated with being negative, as in "don't be so critical." However, this is not what we mean here.

critical
A big part of being critical means that you require supporting evidence before you believe statements that seem true.

Basically, being **critical** refers to certain mental habits: not believing statements simply because they *seem* true, requiring evidence to support statements, and recognizing that something might be wrong or untrue until it is *shown* to be true. In short, a critical person is difficult to convince. A critical person is someone who says "show me the evidence, and then, if the evidence is good, and after I've thought carefully about your argument and the points you've made, I'll agree with you—*maybe*."

In both school and the workplace, **critical thinking** skills are some of the most important skills you can have. When you think critically, you are looking for potential problems and flaws in arguments—for example, lack of evidence. If this definition still sounds negative, you can think of critical thinking as a method for testing arguments to make sure they work, and if they don't work, it's a method for improving them so that they do work.

Such testing is very important. Poorly tested arguments can result in poor decisions, and poor decisions can result in serious problems, either immediately or later on. To prevent such problems, you use your critical thinking skills in advance.

Here's an example. Have you ever made a decision that did not work out as planned? Everyone on Earth, including the authors of this book, would have to answer "yes"!

For example, have you ever

- underestimated how much something was going to cost and run out of money as a result?

- assumed people would react a certain way and then discovered their reactions were totally different from what you expected?

- forgotten about (or ignored) a key detail which interfered with a plan or event?

Good critical thinking skills help prevent potentially serious problems by allowing us to think ahead. Critical thinkers can prevent many negative consequences by identifying potential problems in advance. Of course, no plan is ever perfect, but critical thinking can help *reduce* the chances of failure.

The good news is that critical thinking is a set of skills and habits anyone can learn. In fact, we've been working on many key aspects of **critical analysis**, a related term, since the start of this book. Analysis involves breaking down a complex situation, problem, or text into its component pieces.

Remember that in Module 1.2, we learned how to "break down arguments." The key to success for critical analysis is being able to break down complex arguments into simpler, easier-to-manage elements. When you read through the two essays associated with these modules—and the essays and articles provided to you by your teacher in class—you'll want to consider *what* those writers are trying to make you believe and *how* they are trying to do it.

> **critical thinking**
> Critical thinking requires you to look for potential problems and flaws in arguments—for example, lack of evidence.

> **critical analysis**
> Critical analysis involves breaking down complex arguments into simpler, easier-to-manage elements.

critical response
When you respond to an argument critically, you combine critical thinking and critical analysis.

The *combination* of critical thinking and critical analysis is essential to producing a viable **critical response**, which is your reaction or answer to an argument and to its various main and supporting points. A critical response can be delivered verbally, or it can be written out. Since this is a writing textbook, we will focus on the second option, but for now, let's concentrate on developing critical thinking and critical analysis skills.

Let's look again at Louise Zacarias' "Students Need a Gap Year" on page 8. Here are some questions that you should answer for yourself in preparation for writing a critical response to her argument:

- What do you think of her claims that students are too immature to go directly from high school to college/university?
- Do you think a year off between high school and college/university will actually make any difference?
- Does she provide any evidence for her points?
- What sorts of evidence would she need to support these points?
- Would all students be able to afford a "gap year"?
- Do universities/colleges have the right to restrict their admission requirements in this way, merely to attempt to control the maturity of their students?
- Can you think of any negative consequences to Zacarias' proposal that she does not foresee?

As you were reading through Zacarias' essay the first time, you probably thought of many objections to her statements. Those objections, coupled with the answers to the questions above, demonstrate your critical thinking abilities.

One of the most important characteristics of a good critical thinker is the ability to avoid believing a statement just because it *seems* true. In other words, it's good to doubt reasonably.

It's also possible—and bad—to doubt *unreasonably*. When a writer provides a well-developed and well-supported argument, there comes a point when a critical reader needs to accept the claims made by the writer or prove an alternative theory. Critical thinking is more than just disagreeing with everything we see or hear: it means that we must test the writer's claims, not just accept them at face value.

For now, though, the big point is this:

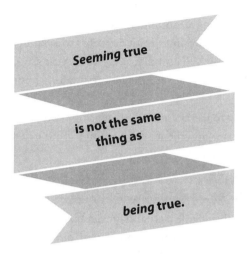

Seeming true

is not the same thing as

being true.

For centuries, people believed that the Earth was flat—and that the Sun travelled around the Earth—because it *seemed* to be that way. Of course, we know now that the Earth is round and orbits around the Sun, but it took a lot of accumulated evidence to establish these facts. The problem with believing something is true because it seems to be true is that we are basing our judgment only on appearance rather than the reality of a situation.

Sometimes our worst decisions are based on statements we refuse to question because these statements already fit with how we think things work. To avoid bad decisions and failed plans, we need to dig a little deeper—it's almost always easier to do some critical thinking earlier than it is to pick up the pieces of a failed plan later.

If a claim *seems* true to you, it might actually be true. Then again, it might not be. Until you have good supporting evidence, as suggested above, you *don't know*, so until you see the evidence, the *most* that you can say is that the claim seems **plausible** or **implausible**.

Implausible is obviously the opposite of *plausible*, but what does *plausible* actually mean? Based on the context of the previous paragraph, you might notice that the word has something to do with appearance. If you look up the word *plausible* in the *Concise Canadian Oxford Dictionary*, you'll see various meanings including "seeming reasonable, believable, or probable."

plausible and implausible
A statement is plausible if it initially seems reasonable or believable. A statement is implausible if it initially seems unreasonable or unbelievable.

Although we can decide that a claim made by an author *appears* to be believable or probable—or even true—we also cannot stop our critical thinking there. Whenever you are making an argument, or responding to an argument made by someone else, there are two important concepts to keep in mind: **supporting evidence** and plausibility. Plausibility is an important aspect of critical thinking, but plausibility alone is never sufficient for crafting a critical response.

supporting evidence
Supporting evidence includes the examples, facts, and statistics that a writer uses to support his or her argument.

Understanding how to use these two concepts is essential for making effective arguments and counter-arguments. Let's examine both in detail.

Supporting Evidence

Arguments frequently include factual claims. A fact can be defined as something which can be objectively confirmed or measured, often an object but sometimes an event or action. For instance, Louise Zacarias in "Students Need a Gap Year" makes this factual claim:

> Currently, more than 50 per cent of all incoming first-year students to Canadian universities are seriously unprepared to manage the stress levels they encounter.

If you came on this sentence all by itself in an argument, it would be, as it stands here, an *unsupported* claim. If someone makes a statement like this, he or she must provide information about the *source* of this knowledge.

If a factual claim like the one above is *unsupported*, it does not mean the claim is false. It may be true, but you have no way of knowing unless you can consult the evidence yourself, or at least have the possibility of doing so. Any argument that relies on unsupported factual claims is a weak argument, and critical, reasonable decision-makers will reject any recommendations made on the basis of unsupported factual claims until *support* is provided.

This distinction between supported and unsupported factual claims is something that you should keep in mind whenever you make or assess arguments.

One important note: not all factual claims require supporting evidence. Some factual claims are what we call common knowledge. If someone in an argument observes that water is composed of two hydrogen atoms and one oxygen atom (H_2O), this statement will not require a source because it is something almost everyone knows.

Be careful with common knowledge, however. Sometimes common knowledge is wrong. As we pointed out earlier, there was a time when a flat Earth was considered common knowledge! Use your judgment. If something seems especially obvious, something almost everyone knows and has known for a long time, then treat it as common knowledge, but if it's a special claim about facts that few could know, provide support through a source.

Sometimes factual claims made in an argument fall somewhere between common knowledge and special claims. For instance, someone could make this statement:

> Most students experience some degree of stress when adjusting from high school to new and more demanding college or university work expectations.

As it stands here, this is an unsupported factual claim. Although it is unsupported, it is plausible. You'll recall that another word for *plausible* is *believable*. Most people will feel that they know this claim to be true. It comes close to being common knowledge. We may not know why we know it, but we do, and we find it plausible. However, when we were presented earlier with Zacarias' claim that more than 50 per cent of all incoming students to Canadian universities are unprepared to manage the stress they encounter, we have no reason to think we know this because it is a very specific factual claim that would require accurate and careful measurement involving surveys and complex statistical analysis.

Although we have no reason to believe that 50 per cent of first-year students experience *unmanageable* stress, we do have some reason—based on common knowledge and plausibility—to believe that many new students do show *some* degree of stress. A plausible claim can be accepted as a basis for argument, although some hesitation is still appropriate. However, even if we accept an author's particular claim as plausible, we should not assume that it's true without evidence. Plausible claims can be true, but implausible claims can also be true.

What if someone said the following?

> The great majority of first-year students moving from high school to university experience no stress of any kind.

Probably most people would find this statement implausible, meaning "not believable." This claim would be both unsupported and implausible, the most suspicious kind of claim. Claims like this one are warning signs of a weak argument.

Very specific factual claims should be supported by providing source information. If they are not supported, they may still be true, but in responding to them, you should indicate that they are unsupported, and as a result, weak.

A more general claim might lack supporting evidence but appear plausible. For general claims without support, you should indicate whether you find the claim plausible or implausible and explain why. If you find it plausible, you can temporarily accept the claim and treat it as a potentially legitimate argument. If you find it implausible, you provide your reasons for rejecting it. Remember, even if you find a claim plausible, you will still require that the writer provides you with evidence to support his or her argument.

Generalizations

absolute vs. qualified generalizations
Absolute or sweeping generalizations are usually implausible statements that overly rely on words like *all* or *every*. Qualified generalizations are more likely to be plausible statements that are introduced with words like *many* or *sometimes*.

What we need to know about generalizations is that they are sometimes plausible and sometimes implausible. Here's a good rule of thumb: **absolute** or **sweeping generalizations** tend to be implausible; **qualified generalizations** are more likely to be plausible.

Consider the following statement:

Men hate shopping.

This short sentence is a clear example of an absolute or sweeping generalization. The word *men* here implies *all* men. All it takes is one man to say he likes shopping and the generalization is disproved. However, here is a revised version:

Many men hate shopping.

Probably most people would find this claim plausible, or at least not completely implausible like the absolute generalization that *all* men hate shopping.

In the case of "Students Need a Gap Year," Louise Zacarias begins her argument with the following two sentences:

Eighteen-year-olds are too immature to start college and university right after high school. Eighteen-year-olds are basically children.

Although this claim is longer than "men hate shopping," it is still an absolute or sweeping generalization. This wording implies that *all* incoming post-secondary students are (a) 18 years old, and (b) immature. This is both implausible and easy to expose as false. All you need to disprove this claim is *one* instance of a first-year post-secondary student who is not "immature."

What if Zacarias had begun her article with this sentence instead?

> **Some** first-year students are too immature to handle the pressures of post-secondary education.

The word *some* qualifies or limits the claim. This change makes the statement much more plausible. In any given group of ordinary first-year college/university students, some will be less mature than others. It would be difficult to determine how many students are immature without undertaking a study and without clarifying terms like *mature*, but as a qualified generalization, this statement is plausible.

Not all generalizations are false. Nevertheless, absolute generalizations tend to be implausible because only one exception disproves them, and there are very few things that do not have exceptions!

On the left-hand side of the table below, you will see words you should avoid when making a generalized claim about an issue. You should also look out for these words in your own reading because recognizing when an author uses sweeping generalizations is an important step to critically analyzing a text.

In your own arguments, if you need to make a generalized observation, you should consider using the words on the right-hand side of the table. These words will help you to qualify your claims.

Sweeping generalizations		Qualifications
all	in no way	at times
all the time	never	many
always	none	most
constantly	not at all	in general
every	not one instance	some
		sometimes

When we argue with friends or relatives, we may exaggerate our claims with absolute generalizations and words like *always* or *never*. At the time, our strong emotional response has given us the impression that our forcefully argued generalizations have made our argument stronger, but actually we have weakened our main point and made it much easier to disprove.

A good argument makes its claims carefully and cautiously. Instead of *absolute yes/no* thinking where something is either one way or another, we should aim for more *nuanced* thinking where things are sometimes a bit of this and a bit of that.

When it comes to argumentation, words like *many*, *some*, *sometimes*, and other qualifiers are important to keep in mind. Remember Penny's conversation with Leonard at the start of this module: there are almost always more than two *either/or* options!

Evidence

Almost every year for the last two decades, the most-watched drama on American television has been a show about evidence. Primetime TV viewers can't seem to get enough of shows, from *Law & Order* to *CSI* to *NCIS* and all of their spin-offs, where detectives and special agents investigate crimes and chase after the criminals. In order to find who is guilty of the crime each week, the investigators look for **evidence** to prove their case. According to the *Concise Canadian Oxford Dictionary*, the word *evidence* refers to the "available facts" or "circumstances" that support a "belief." In other words, evidence is the collection of supporting points that prove the main point of an argument.

> **evidence**
> Evidence is the collection of facts that support the main point, or thesis, of an argument.

The following chart briefly summarizes some common types of evidence that you will encounter in good arguments. The *lack* of these types of evidence is also significant: if you don't find these types of support in an argument, you should point out their absence.

You should also note that individual areas of study—psychology, history, sociology, philosophy, economics, and so on—all have their own particular types of evidence and ways of constructing arguments. You'll learn more about the discipline-specific types of evidence and argument if you take specific courses in these subjects; for now, we'll discuss evidence more generally.

Type	Description	Things to watch out for
Examples	Examples are signalled by such phrases as *for example* or *for instance*. Sometimes examples can be longer and more detailed. Such examples look like stories. Examples can be very powerful types of evidence, but remember that just because something happened one way in one place at one time, the example does not necessarily reflect a general pattern.	Examples can seem convincing, but you should always ask these questions: • Is the example relevant? • Is the example representative? Everyone has heard about someone who smoked heavily and lived to be very old, but one example does not disprove the general pattern that smoking reduces life expectancy.
Facts	Facts are complicated. Some facts are widely accepted; others are not. Yes, something can be true even if people don't accept its truth. However, the reverse is also true: just because something is widely accepted, it is not necessarily true.	What is presented as a fact can sometimes be debatable, subject to interpretation, and even manipulated to seem like it represents something that it doesn't.
Statistics	Statistics are a type of fact. They can be very powerful types of evidence.	Statistics can be very difficult to interpret unless you have extensive training. In the real world, arguments involving statistics are usually made by experienced researchers, experts with years of training in mathematics and statistical analysis.
Scholarly and academic studies; articles in reputable publications	Reputable publications (both digital and print) are those sources with articles written by authorities known for high-quality work in their subject areas: experts with advanced training in their fields of study. These publications usually include all the other types of evidence listed above.	Unless you are yourself an expert, it can be hard to understand and assess such sources. Also, even experts can be biased, construct poor arguments, and make unsupported claims. Learning to assess sources often requires expertise that requires years of training and study. When confronted with this evidence, remember you should not doubt *unreasonably*. However, you should carefully examine all of the claims. In other words, doubt *reasonably*.

Next we'll look in detail at the first two types of evidence: examples and facts. These two types of evidence will form the basis of most of the argumentative articles that you will see and may also form the basis of most of your critical responses to those arguments.

Examples

Examples are a very powerful form of evidence if they fit the situation. However, poor examples—or poor arguments based on good examples—will expose your argument to reasonable criticism. Here is an example of a poorly constructed argument using an example. Suppose one of your teachers said this to the class:

> I don't know why everyone thought the test was so hard. Several students did very well. For example, one student got 90 per cent, so it can't have been that hard.

Anyone skilled in argumentation and evidence would be very critical of this "example." First, perhaps the student who got 90 per cent is the top student in the class. His or her performance is probably not a good measure of how students *in general* viewed the test in terms of its difficulty.

If you investigated further, you might discover that one student did get 90 per cent, but most students did much worse. In this case, we would say that the student who got 90 per cent is *not representative*: in other words, this example is an exceptional case, and cannot be used as evidence for how most students viewed the test.

On the other hand, the reverse argument can also be faulty:

> Ms. Marshall's test was way too hard. Over half the class failed it!

This example doesn't actually use the phrase *for example*, but it is clear that half the class failing the test is intended as evidence of the test's difficulty. However, what if you learned that a large group of students from this class went to a concert the night before instead of studying? In that case, the example is now out of context: the failure of these unprepared students tells us very little about the difficulty of the test.

Facts—Correct, Incorrect, or Cherry-Picked?

Examples are closely related to facts. An example is usually a type of fact.

Consider this statement of fact:

> Zach failed the quiz.

Now consider this argumentative claim based on that fact:

> Zach failed the quiz. Therefore, he is a poor student.

As we mentioned in the table above, the problem with facts can be how they are interpreted. The above claim isn't just a fact: it's a fact *and* an interpretation. Let's suppose that Zach did indeed fail the quiz. That is a fact. However, does this one isolated, accurate piece of evidence by itself automatically prove that Zach is a bad student?

Building an argument on a faulty *interpretation* of factual evidence can cause serious problems. Suppose we add a prediction to the fact and interpretation above:

> Zach failed the quiz. Therefore, he is a poor student. He will probably fail the course.

Does one failure indicate a general pattern? It might. Then again, it might not, and without additional information, we do not know.

Suppose you investigated this claim, and discovered the following additional facts:

> Zach failed the quiz on Monday because he was called in to work on Sunday night and didn't have time to study. However, there have been five quizzes so far in the course, and Zach has done very well on all the other quizzes. His marks are as follows: 90 per cent, 85 per cent, 70 per cent, 95 per cent, and 40 per cent (the one he failed). In addition, the teacher for this course drops the lowest quiz mark, so only the four highest marks count.

If you do the math, you will see that Zach's overall average on the five quizzes is 76 per cent. If you then consider that the teacher drops the lowest mark (the failing grade of 40 per cent), Zach's average on the quizzes is actually 85 per cent. Does Zach still look like a bad student who will fail the course? This example illustrates the danger of picking out a single fact and making an argument based on it without looking at the context, or larger picture.

This type of faulty argumentation is sometimes called "cherry-picking," which means making an argument based on a limited number of facts, sometimes only one. Such poorly chosen, misinterpreted facts make for flawed arguments and incorrect conclusions.

In the table above, we also briefly looked at statistics and studies. In much the same way that examples or facts can be used or misused, statistics and studies often depend on context. It is essential to watch carefully for the interpretations and the predictions that are made on the basis of these types of evidence. You will often see faulty claims built upon a foundation of an actual fact, an accurate statistic, or a reasonable quotation from an authority on a particular subject.

Types of Criticism

Earlier in this module, we talked about combining critical thinking and critical analysis to help you formulate your critical response. We are now going to look at the types of criticisms that you should look for when you are analyzing an argumentative piece of writing. Remember, analysis involves breaking down an author's claims into their component parts. When you break down an author's argument, you will be able to use these critical skills to identify weaknesses in reasoning.

Evidentiary Criticisms

Think back to our example of popular police dramas on TV. In order to find out who commits the crime each week, the investigators search for evidence to support their theories. When they have enough of the right kind of evidence, they make an arrest.

However, if the detectives don't have enough evidence to convict the accused criminal, the prosecutors will send them back out to collect more. If you are about to start a court case, you want to make sure that the evidence that you have is accurate and complete.

The word *evidentiary* comes from the word *evidence*. When you point out that statements in an argument lack evidence, or if you criticize how the author is using particular evidence, you are making what is called an **evidentiary criticism**.

evidentiary criticism
Evidentiary comes from the word *evidence*. You are making an evidentiary criticism when you point out that an author has not used—or has misused—supporting evidence to back up his or her claims.

Let's consider "Students Need a Gap Year" once again. Does Zacarias provide any evidence? She makes a lot of claims, yes, but does she support them with evidence? Specifically, does she give any examples, does she present any facts, or does she cite any statistics or studies?

She does give one cherry-picked example, that of Prince William, and she does make a lot of factual claims: specifically, she claims that students are "immature," that they lack key skills needed to succeed at college or university, and that a year off will fix these problems.

There are several problems with Zacarias' evidence here. First, she cites no support for any of her claims, and in fact, her assertion that all students are immature is an unsupported, sweeping, and implausible generalization. She cites no studies on whether gap years have been shown to improve student maturity. Prince William's gap year is not a particularly good example for regular students. The vast majority of students lack Prince William's financial resources, and none are in line to become King of England!

Practical Criticisms

When you ask how something is going to work, you are asking a practical question. Sometimes the term *logistical* is used to describe these kinds of questions. If you are able to formulate reasonable questions about the practicality of a given idea, you are engaging in **practical criticism**.

Zacarias' use of the example of Prince William in her discussion of gap years indirectly suggests a key practical criticism that you might make of her argument. As we mentioned before, Prince William is not a particularly good example of a typical first-year post-secondary student.

You can make a practical criticism by imagining what kinds of problems might be created as a result of accepting or applying the proposal. For example, what kinds of practical problems might be created if all students had to take a year off between finishing high school and starting college or university?

One obvious potential problem that you might suggest is financial. Can all students afford to take a year off? Some certainly can, but what about the ones who cannot? There is the counter-argument that students can work during this year; however, what if students cannot find jobs? What if there is a recession? Often during bad economic times, people take the opportunity to go to school when they cannot find jobs, but Zacarias' proposal would restrict this option considerably.

When you start thinking along these lines, you are making practical criticisms.

practical criticism
Questions of practicality are sometimes described as logistical questions. You are making a practical criticism when you point out that an author's claims will not work or are impractical in some other way.

Ethical Criticisms

Aside from the evidentiary and practical/logistical criticisms raised above, there is a third common category to consider in critical thinking: ethical criticisms. In some ways, this third category is the most complicated, but using this type of criticism in your critical responses can be very effective.

The term *ethics*, in general, refers to considerations about whether an action is right or wrong in a moral rather than a factual sense. One key question for an ethical critique is "Is it fair?" When you question whether or not an author's argument is fair, just, or morally correct, you are making an **ethical criticism**. Just as the term *evidentiary* comes from the word *evidence*, the term *ethical* comes from the word *ethics*, which the *Concise Canadian Oxford Dictionary* defines as "a set of moral principles."

ethical criticism
Ethical comes from the word *ethics*, meaning "a set of moral principles." You are making an ethical criticism when you point out that an author's argument is unfair or unjust—or even immoral—to a particular group.

For example, someone could argue that it is not fair for colleges and universities to restrict a student's choice about when to sign up for a program. Students have the right, you might argue, to decide for themselves whether they want to take a year off. You might further argue that anything which restricts a student's choice is unfair.

Of course these points are debatable in ways that some of the earlier points about evidence and practicality/logistics are not. For example, someone might make the counter-argument that colleges and universities *do* have the right to determine their admissions rules because requiring an additional year away is similar to requiring minimum grades or previous personal and/or professional qualifications for admission into certain programs. Because of this potential for debate, ethical arguments are often more complicated and more difficult to support and defend than the first two types of criticism.

The important thing to remember here is that arguments involve give and take, back and forth, arguments and counter-arguments, and responses to counter-arguments. They are more like conversations than speeches.

How Do I Say It? Gambits to Point Out Flaws in Arguments

A gambit is a kind of move or "play" that you can make in argumentation. When you are critically responding to another person's argument, you should always begin by considering how that argument uses evidence.

Here are some standard gambits for critically responding to arguments:

Type of criticism	Gambit	Example
Evidentiary Criticism If you have evidentiary problems with the argument, consider using something like this gambit:	Although ___[author]___ 's argument that ___[point]___ is plausible, ___[author]___ cites no evidence to support it.	Although **Zacarias'** argument that **"more than 50 per cent"** of **new post-secondary students "are seriously unprepared"** is plausible, **she** cites no evidence to support it.
Practical Criticism If you have practical problems with the argument, consider using something like this gambit:	___[author]___ 's proposal is not practical and would thus not actually work. [Then, say why **the author's point** would not work.]	**Zacarias'** proposal is not practical and would thus not actually work. **For example, many students would be out of work during their time away from school, and the delay to their education would be a bigger obstacle than some perceived "maturity" issue.**
Ethical Criticism If you have ethical problems with the argument, consider using something like the following gambit:	Although ___[author]___ 's argument that ___[point]___ is supported with some evidence, it remains unethical for the following reasons. [Then, list the reasons.]	Although **Zacarias'** argument that **restricting post-secondary studies to students who have taken a "gap year"** is supported with some evidence, it remains unethical for the following reason: students should have the right to pursue an education whenever they wish.

Overlapping Critiques and Combo Gambits

Evidentiary, practical, and ethical critiques often overlap. You don't have to pick just one of the gambits listed above. In fact, when you critically analyze actual arguments, you will usually end up using several different gambits in combination. Your critical response to an argument will be strongest when you can identify several different types of problems.

We introduce examples of how to combine different types of critiques into a full critical response in the next module (1.5), where we present the key features of an essay, and in Modules 1.6, 1.7, and 1.8, where we discuss the different parts of essays in detail.

Module Checklist

Have I

- [ ] broken down the author's argument into a main point/thesis statement and supporting evidence? (See Module 1.2.)

- [ ] assessed whether the author's generalized claims are plausible or implausible?

- [ ] noted where the author uses problem words that indicate that he or she may be using absolute or sweeping generalizations (*all*, *every*, *never*)?

- [ ] checked for evidence for the author's claims? Does the author *provide* evidence for his or her claims?

- [ ] checked whether or not the author's examples are representative or cherry-picked?

- [ ] asked whether or not the author's ideas are practical? Are there reasons that the author's ideas will not work if implemented?

- [ ] asked whether or not the author's ideas are fair? Have I thought about possible ethical reasons not to agree with the author's main point?

Looking Ahead

Over the last three modules, you have learned how to summarize and respond critically to an argument. How do these skills relate to what comes next? This question has two answers: one short term, the other long term. We'll deal with the long-term answer first.

Critical thinking is a key concept for almost all academic work, so the rest of this book requires that you apply the ideas from this module. More importantly, once you go beyond this book, you'll find that all college and university courses require critical thinking: whenever you do course readings, whenever you write essays, whenever you do research for a research paper, you will need to engage in critical thinking.

Critical thinking is crucial outside of the post-secondary classroom as well. It is an essential *life* skill. We live in a world filled with media messages telling us to buy certain things or think certain ways. Many of these messages attempt to persuade us to make decisions uncritically. When we break down exactly what we are being sold and told, we are thinking critically, and we will be much better informed as a result.

The critical thinking advice in this module is fairly general. You will find that the specifics of critical thinking vary from one course and field to another: for example, psychology courses will not deal with critical thinking in exactly the same way that business courses do. There will still be evidentiary, ethical, and practical questions, but they will change according to the field. Nonetheless, this module provides a solid foundation for your skills as you move into these areas.

How does all of this relate to writing essays? The rest of Part 1 is about how to take the skills from Modules 1.2, 1.3, and 1.4 and apply them to different kinds of essays. Here's how the upcoming Part 1 modules will develop the skills that you will need to become a better writer.

The next module, Module 1.5, provides an overview of the basic features of essays: introductions, bodies, conclusions; it also discusses different types of essays and other types of writing you'll have to do in your college or university courses. You may feel you know all of this material already, but be careful: although you probably know *some* of it, students in college and university are often surprised when gaps in their knowledge show up. Often these gaps appear in the form of lower-than-expected grades on essays, especially in those first few writing assignments for students new to post-secondary education, so please take this material seriously.

Review is always good. After all, when was the last time you wrote an essay? A few months ago? Even longer? Skills can get rusty. In addition, if you do have gaps in your awareness of essay writing, when would you rather find out—now, or after your teachers have graded your work?

Modules 1.6, 1.7, and 1.8, in turn, expand on Module 1.5's discussion of introductions, bodies, and conclusions. Module 1.5 provides an overview of the big picture, but these modules zoom in on the details—and there are a lot of details! Module 1.9, the last module in Part 1 of this book, provides tips on how all of the previous material in Modules 1.2 to 1.8 relates to a different kind of essay-writing scenario: writing essays in exam situations.

Self-Check 2

Refer back to the first self-check at the beginning of this module. Have your ideas changed? What new ideas do you have? Write them out in the chart below.

Based on the objectives at the start, how have my views changed since the beginning of this module?	What new information do I have?

Activities

Before turning to the next module, check your understanding of the concepts and terms of this module by completing the activities below.

1. Look up the words *critical, judgment, evidence/evidentiary, practical,* and *ethical* in the dictionary (any good dictionary will be fine) and compare the definitions you find to the discussion in this module.

   Note on a separate sheet of paper or word-processing document any words used in the definitions that you could use in your own critical response essays. Later in this activity sequence you'll be asked to critically respond to argumentative statements, so keep this list handy.

2. (a) What other words mean much the same thing as *plausible* or *implausible*? List as many different words as you can, and keep this list with the one you made in Activity 1.

   (b) Read Mae Agnesi's "The Future = Math Required" on page 10 or another essay or article given to you by your teacher. Respond to the claims made by the author by using this formula as a basic framework:

   <u>[Author name]'s</u> claims are <u>[alternative word for *plausible/ implausible*]</u> because _____.

3. Read the following six sentences. Each is a generalization. Identify whether it is an absolute/sweeping generalization or a qualified generalization by putting "A/S" or "Q" in the blank provided. If the sentence is an absolute/sweeping generalization, rewrite it using qualifying words. You might wish to consult the "Qualifications" column in the table on page 53 for some word choice suggestions.

   a) Everyone agrees that the Canadian government should raise the income tax rates of the wealthiest 1 per cent of Canadians. _____

   b) You are constantly complaining about the pain in your lower back! _____

   c) Many people believe that baseball players who used performance-enhancing drugs should be banned from the Hall of Fame. _____

   d) Lululemon never puts anything on sale! _____

e) Some big food manufacturers are now focusing on organic versions of popular brands. _____

f) All scientists agree that the dinosaurs were wiped out by a giant comet. _____

4. Sort the statements below into two categories by putting "a" or "b" in the blanks provided:

a) statements that require evidence/support

b) statements that are generally accepted facts and don't require specific support

Note: Not all the statements are necessarily true; some may be plausible but not true, and some may be true but implausible. Also, please note that the correct category for some may be debatable.

i. St. Patrick's Day is on March 17. _____

ii. More and more students with university degrees are going to college after graduation to obtain more technical, job-focused skills. _____

iii. Pink Floyd's 1973 album *The Dark Side of the Moon* is the best-selling album of all time. _____

iv. Stephen Harper became prime minister of Canada on 6 February 2006. _____

v. The winter of 2011–2012 was the warmest winter on record. _____

vi. With multiple-choice questions, your first impression about the right answer is usually the right one. _____

5. The following critical statements are all possible phrases that you could use in a critical response essay. Sort the statements into the following categories: evidentiary criticisms, ethical criticisms, and practical criticisms. Identify them in the blanks provided.

a) . . . students should not have to . . . _____

b) . . . would not work because . . . _____

c) . . . fails to provide evidence . . . _____

d) . . . it is unethical . . . _____

e) . . . no one has the right to force/require . . . _____

f) . . . there is no evidence for the claim that . . . _____

g) . . . has the following problems with evidence . . . _____

h) ... would be unlikely to work because ... _____

i) ... lacks evidence for ... _____

j) ... is impractical because ... _____

k) ... it is unfair ... _____

6. Look again at "The Future = Math Required" (on page 10). Identify the problems in Agnesi's argument, and sort these problems using the table below.

Evidentiary problems	Practical problems	Ethical problems

7. Write out one criticism of Agnesi's piece from each column in the table above. You should try to use the gambits from the table on page 61 of this module to help you with the wording of your criticisms.

8. Evidentiary criticisms, practical criticisms, and ethical criticisms are common parts of real-world arguments. Google these phrases. What do you find? How do your findings relate to the criticisms you're learning to make here? Are there any differences?

9. Your teacher will distribute an article for you to work on. In one paragraph, critically respond to the author's argument. You should try to incorporate words from Activities 1 and 2 in this sequence as well as gambits from the table on page 61.

What Is an Essay, and Why Should I Care?

[MODULE **1.5**]

What Is an Essay, and Why Should I Care?

Module Objectives

Upon successful completion of this module, you will be able to

1. define the term *essay*
2. describe generally the various types of essays commonly written in college and university courses
3. define the key elements of an essay, including the terms
   a) *introduction*
   b) *body*
   c) *conclusion*
4. critique common myths regarding essays
5. explain how reading and responding to texts, in general terms, is related to essay writing
6. reflect in detail about how your existing knowledge about essay writing has changed as a result of reading this module

---

Self-Check **1**

Read the module objectives above. You've probably encountered some of these terms and concepts before; others, however, will likely be new. In point form, identify what seems familiar and what seems new to you in the chart below.

What do I already know about the topics in this module's objectives?	What seems new to me?

What Is an Essay?

The term *essay* is fairly general. The word *essay* originally comes, as most textbooks will tell you, from the French verb *essayer*, meaning "to try." In an essay, you are trying to express an idea effectively in writing. However, what exactly are you trying to do?

The answer depends on the type of essay you write and your purpose for writing it. This module gives you general information about different types of essays commonly required in college and university courses, what your teachers expect, how you can become better at writing essays, and finally, and most importantly, why you should care.

Why You Should Care about Essays

Now

Many college and university teachers devote a lot of marks to essay questions on exams as well as essay and essay-type assignments done out of class, because such questions are more effective than almost any other type of assignment for telling teachers whether students fully understand the material.

Think back over the last few modules. You learned that essays allow students to prove that they can explain the main point/thesis and supporting points of course readings, and even more importantly, allow them to prove that they can deal critically with these readings. After all, if you think about it, there is no better way to prove that you understand something than having to explain it in detail to someone else. Essays allow you to do exactly that.

Later

Although few jobs require that people write essays, you will use the same skills—understanding main and supporting points, using signal phrases, critical thinking, writing clear sentences, and writing well-designed paragraphs—in workplace writing as well. Whenever you write emails, reports, or other work-related texts, you need to have good skills in these areas. In addition, in today's economy, more and more people are returning to school later in life, so your essay writing may not be over just because you've graduated and gotten a job—you might have more schooling in your future.

Types of Essays

Here are some different types of essays that you might be asked to write in college or university courses:

- **literary essays** in which you analyze novels, plays, poetry, or short fiction
- **essays** in which you will have to analyze a text and construct an argument about it
- **personal essays** (less common than the other types) in which you reflect on an issue from your own perspective
- **research essays** in which you will have to narrow down a topic, do research, and assemble your research into an argument about the topic. This type of essay is extremely common.

Note that these types of essays occur more often in certain kinds of university and college courses: English, writing, sociology, history, philosophy, media studies, political science, women's studies, art history, and so on.

If you're taking a technical or professional communications course (which is more common at college than university), you will probably have to do the following kinds of writing, all of which prepare you for workplace writing:

- **technical reports** that require research and present information about a specific professional topic in an organized way
- **responses to proposals** that outline a course of action and may include a specific recommendation
- **instructions** that explain how to do something
- **memos/emails** that communicate specific information about a particular topic
- **cover letters** that accompany resumes in job applications

In addition to these kinds of writing, you may also have to write various other specialized documents, depending on your program. Although these documents are not essays, they still use many features of essays, and if you develop strong essay-writing skills, you will be able to adapt these skills to these documents as well.

For all of these reasons, essay-writing skills are particularly useful, regardless of what you're studying.

Anatomy of an Essay

Most types of writing consist of sentences, which are grouped into larger units called paragraphs. Because the term *sentence* requires a technical definition that is the subject of a separate module (2.1), we're going to start with the term *paragraphs*.

In high school, you almost certainly learned that an essay has three main parts:

- Introduction
- Body
- Conclusion

Introductions

We have already dealt with introductions: when you're writing an essay responding to another text, your introduction should usually begin by establishing the context for what you're saying. For example, if you're responding to something else, you should name and identify the text to which you are responding.

Here is a basic template for writing an introduction to a critical response essay:

1. Identify the title and author of the text that you've read, and summarize its key points (see Module 1.3)
2. Clearly state your critical response to the author's argument (see Module 1.4)

Together, these two initial tasks set up the rest of the essay, in which you provide your own more detailed supporting points for your response argument (see Module 1.7). Meanwhile, Module 1.6 is all about how to write introductions, and we will provide more details then.

Myth, Busted: You Should *Not* Begin with a Generalization

Many students believe they should begin essays with general, sweeping statements about life, society, history, literature, art, or some other area of human experience. However, generalizations rarely make good beginnings for essays.

Think of the opening line of your essay as a "hook": it needs to grab the reader's attention. It also needs to introduce the essay topic, which must be manageable in an essay of the required length. College and university essays range in length from approximately 2 to 30 pages, depending on the subject and the level of the course. A two-page essay isn't long at all, and a 30-page essay, while it may seem long, is still not long enough to properly address an extremely general opening statement about all of human history. A clear and specific opening hook to your essay will help you to develop a focused argument that is appropriate for the word count that you've been assigned.

Specifics can often hook readers; generalities usually don't. A well-chosen and properly integrated quotation from a text relevant to your topic is often an excellent way to begin. For example, if you are trying to respond to Mae Agnesi's article "The Future = Math Required," a broad generalization such as "Throughout history, math has been an important subject for students to learn" is not contributing anything to your overall argument. Instead, we recommend that you select a notable, representative quotation to immediately focus your reader's attention on the issue at hand:

> In "The Future = Math Required," Mae Agnesi argues that "we should require that all college students—regardless of their program—take math courses."

Myth, Busted: You *Can* Start an Essay with a Quotation

This last point about avoiding generalizations relates to another myth: sometimes students think that introductions cannot start with quotations. They can. You don't *have* to start with a quotation, but it's certainly an option. In fact, a lot of essay-writing myths turn options—things you can do or not do, depending on the situation—into absolute rules. We'll discuss more of these options in Module 1.6, which specifically addresses introductions.

Myth, Busted: Your Thesis Statement *Can* Be Several Sentences

Another common myth involves thesis statements. First, a thesis statement does not have to be a single sentence. Sometimes it is; sometimes it isn't. In fact, some of the best essays have multi-sentence thesis statements that lead a reader through the argument of the rest of the paper in a few sentences. After all, that's the purpose of introductions: to set up the rest of the essay.

For example, if you wanted to respond to Louise Zacarias' article "Students Need a Gap Year," you might want a pair of sentences to outline the flaws in her piece and explain the action that we should or should not take:

> Zacarias' proposal has serious evidentiary, ethical, and practical flaws, so colleges and universities should reject this proposal in its current form. However, because some students experience stress when they first enroll in post-secondary education, these schools should carefully research possible solutions to help students manage stress effectively.

If you have been assigned to write a much longer paper, you may find that even more sentences are required to really outline the key points you are trying to make in your argument.

Technically, it's even a myth that the thesis has to be in the introduction: some skilled writers delay their thesis until the end. However, we recommend that you avoid this technique until you have a lot of experience with the more common pattern in which the thesis appears in the introduction.

Body Paragraphs

The body of an essay usually has more than one paragraph. If you're writing a very short essay, you might have a single-paragraph body, but it's usually better to have several paragraphs to develop your points.

Exactly how many body paragraphs should you have? Unfortunately, there is no right answer to this question: it depends on what you are planning to say.

Each paragraph in your body section should begin with an effective topic sentence that sets out what you're going to talk about in the rest of the paragraph. Composing topic sentences helps you to break down your thesis into manageable pieces that can be explored in the body paragraphs. Each topic sentence acts as a "mini-thesis" for the rest of the paragraph that follows. Good topic sentences are like bridges: they connect your thesis in the introduction to the more detailed presentation of points to support your thesis in each body paragraph.

Because they are so important, topic sentences can be tricky to write, but fortunately, there are some rules that you can use to make sure that you write topic sentences effectively. We'll talk about body paragraphs and topic sentences in particular detail in Module 1.7.

Myth, Busted: An Essay Does *Not* Have to Have Five Paragraphs

Although five paragraphs is a convenient pattern for a short essay, allowing for an introduction, three body paragraphs, and a conclusion, an essay does not *require* five paragraphs. As suggested above, the minimum number of paragraphs for an essay is three, but an essay can have any number of paragraphs beyond that, within reason.

Instead of thinking that an essay has to have a certain number of paragraphs, think of an essay as a machine for saying what you want to say. How many parts does a machine need? The answer is this: as many as it needs to work properly, no more and no less.

Myth, Busted: An Essay Does *Not* Have to Have Three Points

A closely related myth is that an essay has to have three points. Although three is also a very convenient number, the number of points you make depends on your argument and your subject matter. Having three paragraphs and three supporting points has been a standard model in colleges and universities for many years. You should know about this rough guideline; however, you should not let it restrict your ability to build a solid argument.

Instead of deciding beforehand on a certain number of paragraphs, let the structure of what you want to say determine the number of paragraphs—but remember that you will commonly need at least three, to match up with the introduction/body/conclusion pattern!

Conclusions

In some ways, conclusions are the easiest sections to write because by this point, you've already stated your thesis and developed your points to support it. For short essays of the sort that we're emphasizing here, the simplest and easiest way to conclude is to restate your points briefly.

For some types of essays, conclusions are more complicated, and we'll discuss these types of writing in Module 1.8.

Myth, Busted: Your Conclusion Does *Not* Have to Begin with *In Conclusion*

The transitional phrase *in conclusion* can work as a basic way to introduce a conclusion, but it is not required. Better, more innovative conclusions often begin in other ways—see Module 1.8 for some suggestions.

Myth, Busted: Your Conclusion Does *Not* Have to Repeat Your Introduction

Repeating the introduction is a quick and easy way to structure a conclusion. However, it's not required, and there are other ways to write conclusions—see Module 1.8 for some suggestions on how you can use a "look-ahead" conclusion or, better yet, a "look-both-ways" (combo) conclusion.

Myth, Busted: Your Conclusion *Can* Introduce a New Idea

Generally, a conclusion should not go off on a completely new direction from the rest of the essay, but it can explore new territory by suggesting a new course of action, presenting a quotation or anecdote or idea for the first time, and so on—again, see Module 1.8 for some suggestions.

Some More General Myths, Busted

There are many more general myths about essay writing. Below, we will show you what's wrong with these myths and provide some suggestions for what you *should* do now that you aren't constrained by these myths.

Myth, Busted: Your Grade Is *Not* Based on Length

Your teachers will give you word counts, and if your essay is much shorter than the suggested length, you'll probably lose marks. They also won't like it very much if your paper is much longer than it's supposed to be. Although there are exceptions, most of your teachers are much less interested in essay length than you may think. They're mainly interested in how good your essay is. In other words, quality beats quantity. A better-written paper at the lower end of the word count will almost always get a higher grade than a weaker paper at the upper end.

Myth, Busted: Your Teacher Does *Not* Usually Want General Information about a Topic

In short-answer questions on quizzes, tests, and exams, your teachers may want you to prove your knowledge of a subject. Essays, however, are more about analysis, argumentation, critical thinking, and good writing skills. Teachers mainly want you to show that you can present and organize your ideas effectively. Depth is more important than surface information: a set of disconnected, random facts will almost always get a lower grade than narrower but deeper analysis.

Module Checklist

Can I

☐ describe what my teacher wants when he or she assigns me an "essay"?

☐ explain what may be required of me when I've been assigned different types of writing assignments in my classes?

☐ identify a number of essay-writing myths that I have heard over the years and disregard them in favour of better advice?

☐ identify the modules in this book that provide extra help in writing effective

    ☐ introductions?
    ☐ body paragraphs?
    ☐ conclusions?

☐ apply the advice given earlier in the book about how to critically read and respond to a text when I'm asked to write an essay?

Looking Ahead

This module is itself basically an overview of the rest of Part 1 of this book, so all of the topics that we have addressed in it look ahead to upcoming modules. More specifically, you'll find much more detailed explanations of the different components of an essay in Module 1.6 (introductions), Module 1.7 (body paragraphs), and Module 1.8 (conclusions).

Self-Check 2

Refer back to the first self-check at the beginning of this module. Have your ideas changed? What new ideas do you have? Write them out in the chart below.

Based on the objectives at the start, how have my views changed since the beginning of this module?	What new information do I have?

Activities

Before turning to the next module, check your understanding of the concepts and terms of this module by completing the activities below.

1. What do you know about essay writing from past courses? Write a brief list of different pieces of helpful advice that you have received about essay writing. Be careful *not* to reproduce any of the myths that we have busted in this chapter!

2. How many of the different types of writing named in this module have you produced in other courses, either previous ones or ones that you're doing now? List them, and briefly note how the points in this chapter relate (or don't relate) to them.

3. a) Sort the following statements into the chart on the next page:

    i. Thesis statements should never be more than one sentence.

    ii. Conclusions should never introduce new information.

    iii. One of several options for writing a conclusion is to restate earlier material, but it's not required.

    iv. One option for establishing context in an essay is to begin with a quotation.

    v. An essay has a minimum number of three paragraphs, but does not have to have five paragraphs.

    vi. Conclusions may begin with *in conclusion*, but they don't have to do so.

    vii. Essay expectations can vary depending on the field of study.

    viii. You should always begin essays with sweeping generalizations about big topics (human existence, history, and so on).

    ix. Grading isn't based mainly on length: quality usually beats quantity.

    x. The best way to get a good grade is to give the teacher as much general information about a topic as possible.

Myths	Truths

b) Once you've completed the chart, check your answers with a partner, and discuss them.

4. Your teacher will assign each student a particular essay-writing myth from this chapter. Working in pairs, "bust" the myths you have been assigned: take turns explaining to each other what is wrong with the myth, and then write down what advice you should follow instead.

How to Write an Introduction

[M O D U L E **1.6**]

How to Write an Introduction

Module Objectives

Upon successful completion of this module, you will be able to

1. write effective introductory paragraphs for short critical response essays

2. explain how introductions may vary for other types of essays

3. outline the key elements required in an introduction to a critical response essay

4. incorporate material from previous modules into introductory paragraphs for critical response essays, including

   a) main/supporting point identification
   b) signal phrases
   c) direct quotation/paraphrase/summary
   d) critical thinking/analysis

5. write effective critical response thesis statements

Self-Check 1

Read the module objectives above. You've probably encountered some of these terms and concepts before; others, however, will likely be new. In point form, identify what seems familiar and what seems new to you in the chart below.

What do I already know about the topics in this module's objectives?	What seems new to me?

Introductions

Imagine reading an essay that starts like this:

> Since the dawn of time, parents have always thought their children were less mature than they actually are. Students don't need a year off, because they are adults. Eighteen-year-olds are basically children, she says, but she is wrong. According to the law, eighteen-year-olds can vote, they can drive, they can serve in the military, and so on, so they are not children in terms of their age. Students shouldn't have to take a year off before they go to college or university. The author says that they should, but she is wrong. At that age, students are mature enough to live on their own. They have often had jobs in high school and they have dealt with the deadlines before, so they do have time-management skills. She overgeneralizes about students by saying that they are all immature. She should reconsider her idea.

Is this a good introduction? Any college or university teacher would say no. This answer raises additional questions. First, why isn't it good? Second, what is good? Third, and most importantly, why do we consider some types of introductions bad and others good?

The following table outlines many of the problems with the introduction above:

Original text	Explanation of problem
Since the dawn of time, parents have always thought their children were less mature than they actually are.	The opening sentence is much too general. Do you know for sure that parents have always thought this way? They may have, but is there proof? If there is, the author doesn't provide it. In fact, proving a statement about all of human history would be close to impossible: it isn't worth it to even try. Remember from Module 1.4 that you should be very cautious about absolute or sweeping generalizations (see pages 52–54).
Students don't need a year off, because they are adults.	Although much more specific, the second sentence seems to come out of nowhere. The idea of students taking a year off isn't introduced properly. How do we go from an unproven, sweeping generalization about parents, children, and maturity to the idea of taking a year off? A year off from what? This problem would have been addressed if the first sentence of the introduction had properly established a context for the response by specifying the author and main point of the text under discussion. A few sentences later, we discover that "a year off" refers to a year off between high school and college/university, but we should not have had to wait so long to find out that that's what this writer meant.

(Continued)

Original text	Explanation of problem
Eighteen-year-olds are basically children, she says, but she is wrong.	The pronoun *she* is introduced without context. The sudden appearance of the pronoun *she* creates more confusion—who is *she*? We don't know, and the writer doesn't tell us. Furthermore, the phrase "Eighteen-year-olds are basically children" is a direct quotation from Louise Zacarias' original article. As you'll remember from Module 1.3 (pages 34–36), any language borrowed from the original author *must* appear in quotation marks.
According to the law, eighteen-year-olds can vote, they can drive, they can serve in the military, and so on, so they are not children in terms of their age. Students shouldn't have to take a year off before they go to college or university. The author says that they should, but she is wrong.	Although these three sentences do start advancing an argument about how eighteen-year-olds are legally adults, we are still puzzled by who *she* is. All of this is confusing because the reader has no context for any of these ideas. The writer really needs to first *establish a context in the introduction* by following these steps: clearly identifying the source text and its author, then framing for the reader what the original writer's main idea is. At that point the writer can then respond to the source text with his or her own thesis statement.

With the above introduction, readers can *eventually* start piecing the puzzle together: someone has proposed that students be required to take a year off after high school before pursuing further education. However, we don't know who, we don't know why, and we don't know where. In fact, this introduction is confusing and difficult to follow because the writer omits key information while scattering other information throughout the paragraph. In other words, this introduction is "bad" because it's incomplete and disorganized.

Many students write introductions like this one, and they lose marks because of it.

What Should Good Introductions Do?

A good introduction needs to set up the rest of your work. Introductions ought to provide the context for what you are writing. In the example above, the writer doesn't provide enough context for his or her argument because he or she doesn't follow the key principles of introduction writing that we'll discuss throughout this module.

It is important to note here that the title of this module refers to an *introduction* instead of an *introductory paragraph* because an introduction and a paragraph aren't the same thing. The term *introduction* refers to the opening section of any text of any length. A short essay might have a one-paragraph introduction; a longer essay or a book would almost always have a multi-paragraph introduction. For now, though, we are going to focus on introductions for short critical response essays, and these introductions are going to be one paragraph long.

At this point, it is extremely important that you have a good grasp of the material from the earlier modules in Part 1. This module assumes that you know all of this material, so you might want to run through the checklist below to make sure that you're familiar with all the required concepts. If you are uncertain about a particular one, you should go back and take a moment to re-read the previous modules and your notes.

Before reading further, you should be able to

- distinguish between main and supporting points in an argument (Module 1.2)
- distinguish among direct quotation, paraphrase, and summary (Module 1.3)
- use signal phrases (with correct punctuation) to introduce direct quotations, paraphrases, and summaries (Module 1.3)
- critically respond to readings using evidentiary, practical, and ethical criticisms (Module 1.4)

Building on these skills, this module focuses on suggestions for writing introductions to short, critical response essays.

Introductions to longer essays with slightly different purposes will vary from the samples provided here. However, many of the skills used to produce clear introductions in critical response essays can be modified to meet the writing requirements of many of the other types of written assignments discussed in Module 1.5.

The Two-Part Introduction

critical response essay
A critical response essay combines critical thinking with critical analysis to respond to what another writer has written. Refer back to pages 46–50 in Module 1.4 for more details.

Here's the good news: you already know how to write half an introduction. As you know from Module 1.3, summarizing a source text is an important step toward establishing a context for what you are writing. In order to establish context so that the reader knows you're responding to another piece of writing, an introduction to a **critical response essay** will often begin by identifying the source text and briefly summarizing its main points. For this reason, we've covered how to break down and refer to texts already in Modules 1.2 and 1.3.

Here's a sample summary of Louise Zacarias' "Students Need a Gap Year"; you may want to compare this summary to the one that you completed in the activity sequence in Module 1.3 (page 41).

> In "Students Need a Gap Year," Louise Zacarias proposes that "colleges and universities should not admit students directly after high school. Instead, they should require that students take a 'gap year' before signing up for more school." According to Zacarias, "[e]ighteen-year-olds are too immature to start college and university right after high school," and she claims that "more than 50 per cent of all incoming first-year students to Canadian universities are seriously unprepared to manage the stress levels they encounter." In addition, Zacarias asserts that if students took a year off between high school and post-secondary studies, they would have more experience coping with new stresses, which she believes would give students "a year of extra maturity when they finally start school again."

> Remember that square brackets are needed to integrate a quotation when you're changing a capital letter to a lower-case one. It is crucial that you absolutely accurately copy your quotation word for word; any changes to the original, including making a capital letter into a lower-case one, must be identified for your reader.

The first major part of an introduction to a critical response essay involves exactly this kind of summary of the source text's main and supporting points. Think of the first part of the two-part introduction as telling your reader what the author has written in the original article.

Next, though, within the introduction, you need to make the kind of critical objections that we discussed in Module 1.4. An introduction is not complete without this important second part because that is where you will be telling your reader what *your* argument is. In general, here is the usual sequence in a two-part introduction to a critical response essay:

1. establish context for the reader by identifying the source and explaining the argument of the source text using signal phrases, as in the summary above

2. establish your position by stating your critical objections as a clear thesis about the source text

As we mentioned in Module 1.4, your critical response will be most clearly articulated in a main point of your own: your thesis statement.

Thesis Statements

Once you have established the position of the author to whom you are responding, it is essential that you establish your own position with a clear thesis statement. The *response* part of the critical response begins with your objections to the original author's claims. Furthermore, in most cases you will want to add an alternative solution to the one presented by the author. We'll discuss how to do that below.

Most students know in general that a **thesis statement** is the place where they should state their overall argument. Remember from Module 1.5, a thesis statement *does not* have to be just one sentence. Sometimes student writers make mistakes with their thesis statements that hurt their essays (and their grades). Here are some common mistakes students make with thesis statements and some ideas on what to write instead so that your thesis can clearly introduce your argument to your readers.

> thesis statement
> The thesis statement clearly presents the overall argument—or main point—in a piece of writing. A thesis statement does not have to be just one sentence.

Avoid the Delayed Thesis

Sometimes students think that they should start a new paragraph for their thesis statement because the shift from summary to the thesis seems like a change in topic. It is, in a way, but in general, you shouldn't start a new paragraph to present your thesis statement. Your summary and your thesis are separate things, yes, but they are also very closely connected because your summary of the original writer's thesis establishes the context for your thesis. In shorter essays, both parts generally should be together in one paragraph—your introduction.

Very experienced, skilled writers can sometimes delay thesis statements effectively, especially for longer essays or even books. Sometimes thesis statements can even go in the conclusion. It takes a lot of skill to break with the conventions, though, and the convention is that the thesis goes in the opening paragraph because it needs to be there in order to set up the rest of the essay for the reader.

Avoid the "Non-thesis" Thesis

Here is an example of a non-thesis type of thesis based on the "Gap Year" article we've been discussing in this module:

> This essay will discuss Louise Zacarias' proposal.

This statement doesn't tell the reader anything about the writer's position regarding Zacarias' arguments. Also, it's usually better to avoid statements like "this essay will discuss ___." Keep the focus on what you're talking about—instead of saying what you're going to say, just say it.

For example, you shouldn't simply promise to discuss, argue, investigate, analyze, elaborate on, or explain something. Write a thesis statement that tells the reader the overall point of the rest of your essay. At times in the writing process, you may wish to use a phrase like "this essay will discuss ___" when you are writing a rough draft, just to help you get started; however, you should make sure to improve on it in the revision stage.

Here is an improved version for our response:

> Zacarias' proposal has serious evidentiary, ethical, and practical flaws.

This sentence is much better because it tells the reader that the writer is going to argue that the proposal has flaws and that these flaws fall into three categories. If you look back at Module 1.4, you'll find an explanation of each of these flaws in Zacarias' essay.

As a quick reminder here, "evidentiary flaws" means that Zacarias does not provide enough evidence to support her argument. Next, "ethical flaws" means that Zacarias proposes a solution to the problem of student readiness that is unethical or unfair to a certain group of people. Lastly, "practical flaws" means that—for a variety of reasons—Zacarias' idea just won't work.

Of course, the thesis statement we've presented above doesn't get too far into exactly what these flaws are—and this observation brings us to our next point.

Avoid the "So-What" Thesis

It's not really enough just to identify problems with another writer's argument. If you have been asked to critically respond to Zacarias' article, you should address her main point: she believes that students should be required to take a mandatory gap year between high school and college/university.

Do you agree with her proposal? If it "has serious evidentiary, ethical, and practical flaws," you should come back to her main point and say that no, students should not be required to take a gap year. Otherwise, you'll leave the reader hanging.

The example thesis statement above might prompt readers to say "so what?" To fix this problem, you can expand the statement by adding some additional information:

> Zacarias' proposal has serious evidentiary, ethical, and practical flaws. Her argument lacks supporting evidence, is unfair to students, and would never work. Therefore, students should not be required to take a year off between high school and post-secondary school.

The two additional sentences improve on the initial version by *briefly* explaining what the three flaws are and then linking back to—and rejecting—Zacarias' main point.

Avoid the Overly Negative Thesis

The revised thesis above is significantly improved, as it now makes specific, debatable claims about Zacarias' proposal beyond simply promising to discuss it. However, it's entirely negative. When possible, it's usually better to move from negative to positive by offering a different, more viable solution to the problem than the one that the original author provided. Thus, instead of simply eliminating the original proposal, you can produce a new proposal that may work better.

Productive Thesis Statements: Moving from Negative to Positive

To move from a negative to a positive thesis, you can use the following techniques. At times it may be difficult to think of an alternative solution. Here is a list of possibilities that you might use to help you come up with a more positive response. You might

- propose an alternative solution to whatever problem the author of the source text is attempting to solve (student problems with math, the need for greater student maturity before starting college, etc.)

- propose that the original author's claims *may be* plausible but that more research be done on the problem (see page 49 in Module 1.4 for a full discussion of plausibility)

- propose that more choice be given to those affected by the problem

Each of these proposals could then link to a body paragraph that would then develop each point in more detail. Any of these bulleted suggestions would help you to smoothly transition into your first body paragraph, which we will discuss more in the next module.

In the case of our sample thesis statement above, you might propose a positive alternative in the following way:

> Zacarias' proposal has serious evidentiary, ethical, and practical flaws, so colleges and universities should reject this proposal in its current form. However, because some students experience stress when they first enroll in post-secondary education, these schools should carefully research possible solutions to help students manage stress effectively.

In this example, we have shortened the negative part of the thesis statement down to the phrase "so colleges and universities should reject this proposal in its current form." Next, we added a sentence that helps us to move from a negative rejection of Zacarias' claims to a productive discussion of what might be done to help those post-secondary students who do experience overwhelming stress when they begin their studies.

You may be thinking that this thesis statement is very detailed, and you're right. If you have the time to work on a thesis statement at home, you could think about possible alternatives to the original author's idea and incorporate those into your essay. Sometimes, though, you'll be asked to write a critical response essay on the spot, and you may find that the negative thesis statement is all you can do. The general idea is that you should always do the best you can in the time you have. Also, keep in mind that you may end up writing a rough draft and then revising it later—we say a lot more about this topic in Module 2.8.

Module Checklist

You will notice here that some of these checklist questions overlap with those in Modules 1.2, 1.3, and 1.4. This repetition is, as you've seen throughout this module, because breaking down an argument, referring to texts, and critically responding all work together to form an introduction in a response essay.

In my introduction, have I

☐ established a context for the reader by providing all necessary information?

☐ worded my opening sentence as concisely as possible?

☐ summarized the main and supporting points of the text to which I'm responding? (See Modules 1.2 and 1.3 if you need to review these points.)

☐ referenced the original author and article using correct signal phrases? (See Module 1.3 if you need to review these points.)

☐ used the correct format for such references? Specifically, have I

   ☐ placed short direct quotations in quotation marks?
   ☐ blocked and offset direct quotations longer than 4 lines or 40 words?
   ☐ paraphrased/summarized—using entirely my own words—for summary/paraphrase? (See Module 1.3 for more information about each technique.)

☐ accurately quoted the original text and placed borrowed language in quotation marks?

☐ presented my own critical thesis about the text to which I'm responding? (See Module 1.4.)

☐ provided *both* a critical summary of the original article *and* a thesis statement of my own?

Looking Ahead

You will use the skills covered in this module to create introductions that successfully do what you want them to do: set up and organize your essay and establish your argument through a thesis statement. Module 1.5 addressed many different types of essays—and other kinds of post-secondary assignments—that you'll be asked to write during your post-secondary education and into your career. Writing a clear and focused introduction will be valuable in all of those writing assignments. Academic writing benefits from a clearly outlined approach to a particular topic, whether it is in a critical response essay, as we've looked at here, or in a research essay for a completely different course. Workplace writing also generally requires a *frontloaded* introduction that lays out for the reader the main point that you are trying to communicate. After all, your boss or your co-workers may have a lot of material to read each day, and they need to know exactly what you are proposing as soon as they look at your writing.

Not all introductions will follow the same format that we discuss here. However, you can certainly transfer and, if necessary, adapt the techniques that we describe here to other writing situations. For example, in a research paper or report, you will not necessarily be responding to a single source. Such papers require that you read and refer to many different sources. However, you may still choose to establish context at the beginning by quoting a particularly relevant source, a passage that sets up the issues of your paper, and so on. As you gain more experience and skill as a writer, you'll gain a better awareness of what works where.

The next module addresses body paragraphs in essays. Your effective introduction has provided the reader with a kind of contract. You've addressed the main idea that you are responding to, and then you've provided the reader with an argument—and maybe even a proposed alternative solution—of your own. It will be your responsibility to pick up where your introduction leaves off and provide supporting evidence for *your* claims. Module 1.7 will explore how best to accomplish this essential task in your essay's body paragraphs.

Self-Check 2

Refer back to the first self-check at the beginning of this module. Have your ideas changed? What new ideas do you have? Write them out in the chart below.

Based on the objectives at the start, how have my views changed since the beginning of this module?	What new information do I have?

Activities

Before turning to the next module, check your understanding of the concepts and terms of this module by completing the activities below.

1. Read and carefully examine the following introductory paragraph of an essay written in response to Mae Agnesi's article, "The Future = Math Required."

    > Math has always been an important part of our society. In Agnesi's article, she argues that colleges should start making math courses mandatory for all students. She says that this idea will help the Canadian economy because there are few careers that don't involve math in some way. This essay will discuss Agnesi's proposal. Math is important, but the author's stance doesn't make sense for everyone. There are many reasons not to do this.

    Does the introduction meet all of the criteria set out in the checklist? Why or why not? Explain in detail, sentence by sentence.

2. Consider some possible introductory sentences to a critical response to Mae Agnesi's article, "The Future = Math Required," in the table that follows. Look carefully at each sentence. Does each one include all of the necessary summary information that we've outlined in this module and in Module 1.3? If not, indicate what information is missing in the third column. Finally, in the last column, rewrite the sentences to add any missing information.

Introductory sentence	Includes necessary information? (Please circle.)	Missing information (if any)? Be specific.	Rewrite the flawed thesis statements to add any missing information.
Mae says that we should all take math, but we shouldn't have to do that.	Yes / No		
Throughout history, humans have used mathematics to help better understand the world.	Yes / No		
In "The Future = Math Required," Mae Agnesi argues that "all college students—regardless of their programs" should be required to "take math courses."	Yes / No		
In the article "The Future = Math Required," Agnesi argues that college students should be forced to take math.	Yes / No		

Introductory sentence	Includes necessary information? (Please circle.)	Missing information (if any)? Be specific.	Rewrite the flawed thesis statements to add any missing information.
In the article "The Future = Math Required," by the author Mae Agnesi, she argues that the colleges should force students to take math courses.	Yes / No		

3. Read each pair of thesis statements below and select the best one. Be prepared to explain to the class why your selection is the best statement. Support your choice with detailed reference to this module. Note, in some cases the best thesis may arise from combining elements of the two statements.

a) I agree and kind of disagree with the writer.

Although Agnesi makes some good points, her overall idea is flawed and should not be implemented.

b) Colleges and universities should reject the writer's claims because of their lack of evidence and impracticality.

Many of the author's points are bad; for example, she writes about one particular student who didn't understand fractions, but that student is just one person.

c) The writer is wrong.

Agnesi's main idea is unworkable and unethical.

d) I hate Agnesi's stupid idea, and I shouldn't have to take math.

Students should have the freedom to select the courses that will best help their future career goals and should not be forced into extra math courses that they may not need.

e) Agnesi's argument has evidentiary problems, including sweeping generalizations about all students' problems with math.

Agnesi has a sweeping generalization.

4. a) Imagine the following situation. Your friend is taking a writing class. You've taken this writing class before with the same teacher, who you know is very particular about introductory paragraph format. Your friend has a draft introductory paragraph due tomorrow. What advice would you give your friend? Be specific!

b) Take your advice from 4(a) and exchange it with a partner in your class. Compare the advice that you gave. Did you give the same advice? What's the same? What's different? Discuss the similarities and differences with your partner.

5. a) The following introductory paragraph is scrambled. Put the sentences in the correct order. Note: there is no single correct order, so your results may vary. The way it currently appears definitely does not work, however.

> She contends that adding more math courses will help our economy because "there are few careers that don't involve math in some way." Perhaps colleges should encourage more students to enroll in math courses, but they should research exactly what kind of math courses would most benefit the students who hope to graduate and get jobs. In "The Future = Math Required," Mae Agnesi argues that colleges should make math courses mandatory for all students, "regardless of their programs." Although Agnesi is right that math is important to Canada's future, her proposal is flawed on practical and ethical grounds. She also presents some flawed evidence to support her points. According to Agnesi, "[s]tudents do not seem to be getting the math they need in high schools."

b) Once you've unscrambled the introduction, identify three features that make the correctly ordered paragraph effective. Write those effective features down and compare your answers with your partner's.

6. a) Your teacher will provide you with a source text in class. Write the introductory paragraph of a critical response to this article. Use the checklist at the end of the module to guide your structure.

Try to write a fully developed introduction because you will be asked to work on this example essay in other activities in this book.

b) Exchange paragraphs with a partner. Make suggestions about each other's work.

c) Revise your introductory paragraph making use of your partner's comments and the list that you created in Activity 5.

How to Write Body Paragraphs

[M O D U L E **1.7**]

How to Write Body Paragraphs

Module Objectives

Upon successful completion of this module, you will be able to

1. explain the purpose of body paragraphs and their relationship to the introduction of an essay
2. write effective topic sentences
3. support the argument made in your body paragraphs using evidence
4. write cohesive, coherent body paragraphs of an appropriate length
5. use transitions and repeated keywords to strengthen the connections between body paragraphs

Self-Check 1

Read the module objectives above. You've probably encountered some of these terms and concepts before; others, however, will likely be new. In point form, identify what seems familiar and what seems new to you in the chart below.

What do I already know about the topics in this module's objectives?	What seems new to me?

Bring In the Evidence: Using Body Paragraphs to Support Your Case

Suppose you are writing an essay that critically responds to Mae Agnesi's "The Future = Math Required"—in fact, you should have already written an introduction responding to this essay in the activities for Module 1.6. Imagine that, after your introduction, your next paragraph reads like this:

> According to Agnesi, because students are bad at math, all students should be required to take math courses in college. Unfortunately, however, Agnesi does not provide any evidence for the claim that students have weak math skills. It is reasonable to assume that some students have weak math skills, but it is not reasonable to assume that all students do. Her suggestion that students in general have weak math skills is in fact a sweeping generalization. Agnesi's proposal also has another major problem: in addition to overgeneralizing about students, she also ignores students' different needs with regard to their math skills. Some students are taking programs that already require math, and other students are taking programs that have different math needs compared to other programs. Without more research to obtain better evidence about how colleges can best meet students' different math needs, colleges should not take her proposal seriously.

This body paragraph has both strengths and weaknesses. Take a moment—do you have any ideas about what they are?

In order to explain, we first have to think about the purposes of body paragraphs and how the paragraph above relates to these purposes.

Body Paragraphs: What They Do and How They Relate to Introductions

Module 1.6 explains how to introduce your essay and how to write a clear and precise thesis statement. You've also seen how to signal to the reader what key points you are going to address in your essay. Next, you need to make your case in your body paragraphs.

In this module, we'll work through the basic structure of body paragraphs systematically. We will outline effective techniques for beginning your body paragraphs, for supporting your claims, and for ensuring that your reader can follow your argument.

The example paragraph above does develop one of the critical response points from Module 1.4: it makes an evidentiary critique and then elaborates on it with several additional points about Agnesi's general lack of evidence, her over-generalizations about students' math skills, and her neglect of students' different needs with regard to math. It ends by pointing out that more research might help the argument but also takes a clear position against Agnesi's proposal in its current, poorly supported form. Assuming that the thesis of the introduction deals with evidence, we can say that the content here is fairly good because it further develops that aspect of the thesis.

However, there is also lots of room for improvement, and the rest of this module uses these areas for improvement to illustrate several important points about writing body paragraphs.

Topic Sentences

topic sentence
A topic sentence is the clear, debatable, and concise sentence that acts as a mini-thesis for your body paragraph.

In Module 1.5 you learned that the first sentence of a body paragraph is called a **topic sentence**. A topic sentence is the clear, debatable, and concise sentence that sets out what you're going to talk about for the rest of the paragraph. You need your topic sentence to bridge the gap between your main point—proposed in your thesis statement in your introduction—and the more detailed points that support your thesis in each body paragraph.

Think of it like this: effective topic sentences help both you as a writer and also your readers. To write good topic sentences, you must start by breaking your argument down into manageable chunks. Having topic sentences helps your reader follow your essay's organization because these sentences indicate how your body paragraphs develop your argument.

The relationship between your thesis and your topic sentences is like the relationship between main and supporting points that we discussed back in Module 1.2. Back then, we dealt with the main and supporting points in the text to which you're responding. Now, you can think of your thesis as *your* main point in response to what you have read, and you can think of your topic sentences in terms of *your* supporting points for your thesis. In fact, if you listed your thesis statement and your topic sentences out by themselves, they should present an outline of your essay.

In other words, if you're writing a critical response to Mae Agnesi, you can think of your thesis as your main point in response to Agnesi's overall argument about why math should be mandatory. Your topic sentences, meanwhile, will support your main point with smaller, more specific points about Agnesi's use of evidence, whether or not you think her proposal is practical, whether or not you think her proposal is fair, and so on.

In this sense, you can think of each topic sentence both as a supporting point for your thesis statement and as its own mini-thesis for each body paragraph. As a mini-thesis, your topic sentence will help define which one of your supporting points the body paragraph will develop.

In our example body paragraph on page 101, we have decided to address the evidentiary problems introduced in Agnesi's poorly reasoned argument, and we have done so by focusing on the math needs of students. Each body paragraph will focus on one key piece of our response to Agnesi's article, so the topic sentence must help us to clearly define which aspect we'll address in the body paragraph at hand.

Here is the topic sentence from the example body paragraph:

> According to Agnesi, because students are bad at math, all students should be required to take math courses in college.

This topic sentence does set up the general topic of the rest of the paragraph, which is about Agnesi's claim that students' general weakness in math justifies a general math requirement in college. However, note that it says nothing critical about Agnesi's claim.

Although the second sentence in the example body paragraph does begin to respond to Agnesi's claims, a topic sentence works best if it *includes a critical statement*. Indeed, it is also essential to remember that the topic sentence *must still be your argument*. In general, it's best not to write topic sentences that solely refer to the other writer's work.

There are several critical statements you can make in response to Agnesi's thesis. For example, Agnesi sweeps *all* students into a single generalization throughout her essay. She makes unreasonable claims about "the education system" on the basis of a single example of one student not understanding percentages: such a cherry-picked example is hardly good evidence for a general argument. Furthermore, Agnesi is unclear about what kinds of math courses she thinks students should take; in fact, she conspicuously neglects to provide such details. Any of these objections to Agnesi's essay could form the basis of a clear and debatable topic sentence.

In order to write good topic sentences, we need to review examples of what works and what does not. Remember our description of a topic sentence: it is clear, debatable, and concise. If a topic sentence isn't all of these three things, then it should be revised.

Here is one possible revision:

> There is insufficient evidence to force all college students to take math courses regardless of the program they are in.

There are both strengths and weaknesses to this kind of topic sentence. It is clearly on topic, debatable, and concise. It indicates that the rest of the body paragraph will deal with the lack of evidence to impose such a large curriculum change. However, one of the weaknesses of this topic sentence is that it doesn't really indicate what the author has said about the topic.

Look again at our example of a weak topic sentence back on page 103: you shouldn't *only* tell your reader what an author said. However, you could address this particular weakness by incorporating a reference to the author's argument into a topic sentence that sets up your own argument in the paragraph that follows.

Here is an example of a topic sentence that does all of this:

> Agnesi provides no evidence to support her idea that all college students should take math courses.

This topic sentence is still very straightforward, but it has added more information. For example, now the name of the author whose article you are responding to is clearly presented. In addition, Agnesi's main point is clearly presented in your own words. Lastly, your argument for the rest of the body paragraph—that Agnesi fails to use sufficient evidence to support her thesis—is clear to your reader.

Once you have learned to write topic sentences that clearly link your own points with the points from the essay to which you're responding, you can experiment with more complex sentence structure. For example, you might indicate what the author says first and then use a semicolon and a transition word to indicate how you are going to respond to that assertion:

> Agnesi contends that all college students should be required to take math courses regardless of their program; however, her argument is flawed because she does not provide enough evidence to support her claims.

This sentence is more complex than the ones above, but notice how it is doing the same thing. It indicates the main point that you are critically responding to, and then it tells the reader how you are going to respond in this body paragraph. For more information about this sentence pattern, you should look at how to use semicolons, which we cover in Module 2.2.

You might also use subordination to get the same idea across:

> Although Agnesi claims that students' poor math skills justify a required math course for everyone, she does not provide any evidence for the claim that students in general have weak math skills.

Just like the example with the semicolon above, the topic sentence here outlines the claims made by Agnesi and indicates how you will respond to them. Note that this revised topic sentence begins with the word *although*. Transition words like the subordinating conjunction *although*, the coordinating conjunction *but*, and the conjunctive adverb *however* (with a semicolon before it) are especially good at joining the original writer's idea to your criticism of that same idea in the same sentence. For more information about these words and how they work in terms of grammar and punctuation, see Modules 2.1 and 2.2.

All of these revised topic sentences—from the simplest to the most complex—improve on the original because they present a unified connection between the two ideas that define the paragraph's subject matter: specifically, they join Agnesi's claim with the response writer's own critical thesis about what Agnesi claims. They are thus better at doing what a topic sentence is supposed to do: setting up the paragraph that follows.

There are other possible topic sentences for a body paragraph, of course. The most important thing to remember is that you need to clearly present a focused mini-thesis for the claims that you are about to make in that paragraph.

Developing Your Point with Evidence

Once you have written an effective topic sentence, you must develop its argument. If you are writing an in-class essay or essay exam, you won't have as much access to external sources of evidence as you would if you've been asked to write an out-of-class research essay.

However, an in-class critical response does give you what the original author wrote, and you can weave that author's points into your own essay. You can write an effective critical response with just the original article or essay if you use the skills that you learned in Modules 1.3 and 1.4 to develop your own logical and well-reasoned points.

If we now add our final revised topic sentence to the next two sentences in our example body paragraph (from page 101 earlier in the module), we get the following group of sentences:

> Although Agnesi claims that students' poor math skills justify a required math course for everyone, she does not provide any evidence for the claim that students in general have weak math skills. It is reasonable to assume that some students have weak math skills, but it is not reasonable to assume that all students do. Her suggestion that students in general have weak math skills is in fact a sweeping generalization.

Note that the two additional sentences do not develop the topic sentence sufficiently. What can be done? Specifically, the writer should develop each of the two sentences with additional discussion and examples. The writer should also explain more about the term *sweeping generalization*. Finally, the writer can use Agnesi's own words as evidence by quoting and then commenting on them, as we suggest in Module 1.3 (on page 33).

Look at the paragraph below. The sentences that we've added to the original example paragraph appear in colour. Note how the additional sentences develop the existing points:

> Although Agnesi claims that students' poor math skills justify a required math course for everyone, she does not provide any evidence for the claim that students in general have weak math skills. It is reasonable to assume that some students have weak math skills, but it is not reasonable to assume that all students do. **For example, Agnesi claims that "students**

do not understand statistics" and "students cannot calculate basic percentages." When she refers to "students," she implies that *all* students have this problem. Thus, this statement is in fact a sweeping generalization. Her argument is unjustified because she relies too much on generalizations about all students, as if all students are the same. Indeed, anyone can easily refute such a claim by finding even a few students who have good math skills.

Note that the last original sentence has been edited slightly to make it fit with the new sentence that now comes before it. These sentences now make a more developed critique of a particular aspect of Agnesi's argument.

It is also often possible to find something good in a writer's argument, and we can also use a quotation to highlight the positive things that another writer has to say. However, even if we plan on agreeing with a point, we must still add something of our own. Just as in the above example, a quotation needs our interpretation; no argument is self-evident.

Perhaps we think that Agnesi makes a valid observation here:

> After all, there are few careers that don't involve math in some way: engineers and computer specialists are obvious examples, but nurses need to know drug dosages, and even people who work in retail or food-service jobs need to do some math, even with computers and cash registers to help them out.

We might look at Agnesi's point here as a reasonable one. First, she doesn't rely solely on generalization: she takes the important step of saying "few" careers do not involve math (rather than an absolute generalization like "*all* careers involve math *all* of the time"). Thus, we could support *some* of Agnesi's argument in our response, while still building on our previous work:

> On the other hand, Agnesi does raise some good points about the importance of math. For example, she notes that "there are few careers that don't involve math in some way." In order to better prepare our students for an economy that demands some math skills, we could make some college-level courses a new priority. However, as we've already seen, it is unreasonable to assume that all students have the same ability level in math, so a new approach to college math would be necessary.

concession
You make a concession when you admit that the writer to whom you are critically responding has made a good point. This admission can strengthen your case by showing your reader that you can see the value of some points even while critically responding to other points.

This passage adds your observation that part of Agnesi's argument does, in fact, make some sense. By showing that you understand what may be good about the source text, you are making a **concession** to some—but not all—of Agnesi's argument. Moreover, in demonstrating that you have the skill to separate the good from the bad in her argument, you are adding something of your own to the debate about the math skills of college students.

Don't confuse making a concession with weakness; it is actually a strength! You can agree with part of what someone says without agreeing to the person's entire argument. For example, you might agree that Agnesi is correct about math being important without accepting Agnesi's sweeping claims about making all students take math in college regardless of their aptitude level.

Yes, you are agreeing with part of Agnesi's argument—just not the flawed parts. In addition, because you have been measured and logical in your response, the reader will be more inclined to accept your criticisms of Agnesi.

Coherence and Length

You may have noticed another weakness about the sample paragraph that opens this module: it seems to switch topics halfway through. The first part is about Agnesi's lack of evidence; this is the part that we have developed so far. The second part, however, is about how her proposal doesn't properly consider students' math needs. These are related topics in the sense that they are both criticisms of Agnesi, but they are different enough that they could be in two separate paragraphs, each with its own topic sentence.

Interestingly, the second half already begins with a sentence that can work as a topic sentence for our next paragraph, and it is already reasonably well developed, so we don't need to change the topic sentence here. However, a little more development of the points that we make would improve our case. One way to further develop a point is to add a pertinent example. We've shown the new sentence that we've added to the original paragraph in colour here:

> Agnesi's proposal also has another major problem: in addition to overgeneralizing about students, she also ignores students' different needs with regard to their math skills. Some students are taking programs that already require math, and other students are taking programs that have different math needs compared to other programs. For example, students studying engineering likely require very different math skills

than students studying to be chefs. Without more research to obtain better evidence about how colleges can best meet students' different math needs, colleges should not take her proposal seriously.

By adding this example, you're developing the point about students' different needs by making it more specific.

Adding an example to help bolster your claims is not the only revision we have made to this body paragraph. Because the original body paragraph dealt with more than one key aspect of our argument, it was not as developed as it could have been. When a body paragraph clearly addresses one particular idea, we say that it is **coherent**, which means that all of the points in the paragraph clearly relate to each other and to the topic sentence.

Coherence is closely connected to length. When a paragraph switches topics halfway through, there will usually be one of two problems: either the two different topics will be undeveloped, or, if they are developed, the paragraph is much too long.

There is no fixed rule about how long a paragraph should be, but a good general guideline is that it should be roughly one-third to one-half of a page, double spaced. Although the same words will take up more or less space depending on whether they're typed or handwritten, if you find that a paragraph is going on for more than half a page, think carefully about whether you should split it into separate parts. You might also be able to make it more concise—for examples of how to do so, see Module 2.7.

> **coherent**
> A coherent body paragraph is easy to follow for your reader because its points all relate clearly and logically both to each other and to the topic sentence.

Cohesion and Transition

Writers should create smooth transitions from one idea to another and one paragraph to another—this smooth flow is called **cohesion**. Cohesive writing is much easier for readers to follow. In fact, using transitions to bring your reader along through your argument has the added value of making your writing seem more persuasive.

Once you have learned to look for cohesion *within* your body paragraphs, you need to check for cohesion *between* your body paragraphs. Remember that cohesive writing helps your reader follow your argument. Because each of your body paragraphs will present one main part of your overall argument, you need strategies to help your reader follow your argument from one point and one paragraph to the next.

> **cohesion**
> Cohesion refers to how well something fits together. Cohesive body paragraphs fit together well and are easy to follow because keywords and transitions help the ideas flow smoothly.

Let's look again at the topic sentence of the example body paragraph on page 108:

> Agnesi's proposal also has another major problem: in addition to overgeneralizing about students, she also ignores students' different needs with regard to their math skills.

The point of this topic sentence is not only to provide a mini-thesis for the rest of the body paragraph, but also to help the reader follow the overall argument by linking back to the previous body paragraph. How do we do that, though? In this one sentence we use both transitions and repeated keywords to improve the cohesion between our paragraphs.

If you look again at the revised example body paragraph that starts at the bottom of page 106, you will find the keywords *sweeping generalization* and *generalizations about all students*. In the new topic sentence on page 108, we repeat the key concept about Agnesi's generalizations, this time using the phrase *overgeneralizing about students*. These repeated keywords remind the reader that Agnesi's argument is flawed and that it overgeneralizes.

Repeating keywords is only one strategy for ensuring cohesion between your body paragraphs. In addition, you can use transition words and phrases to help your reader follow your argument from point to point. In our example topic sentence, we use the transition expression *in addition* to note that there are more problems to be discussed in this new body paragraph. By combining repeated keywords with transitions, we have helped the reader seamlessly flow from one body paragraph into the next.

There are a lot of different transitional words and phrases that you can use to improve a body paragraph's cohesion, but we can narrow down the long list of possibilities to a few helpful examples from our revised body paragraphs on pages 106 and 108:

First paragraph	Second paragraph
For example	also
Thus	in addition to
Indeed	For example

For more information about using transitions to link your sentences and paragraphs together, review the material discussed in Module 2.2. There are also several different kinds of transitional words and phrases that you can use to introduce repeated keywords, so we recommend that you look at Modules 2.1 and 2.2 for examples of what they are and when to use them for maximum cohesiveness.

Module Checklist

In my body paragraphs, have I

- [ ] developed the critical thesis in my introduction with additional supporting points?
- [ ] written topic sentences that clearly outline the relationship among all the points?
- [ ] developed each topic sentence with explanations, examples, and other support?
- [ ] ensured coherence by checking that all my points relate to each other and to the topic sentence clearly and logically?
- [ ] checked to make sure that each is an appropriate length?
- [ ] ensured cohesion by checking that all my points clearly flow together (both within and between paragraphs)?

Looking Ahead

By this point in this book, you have learned techniques for writing introductory paragraphs and body paragraphs. Because an essay in general has three main sections, in a way you're now two-thirds done. The next module, Module 1.8, addresses the final element of an essay: the concluding paragraph. Once you've finished Module 1.8, you will have gone through the full process of learning, reflecting on, and practising writing the basic components of an essay.

You will find that other types of essays, reports, and documents that you may need to write in the future may require slightly different arrangements of these elements than we present here. You should also be aware that the development of your writing skills does not end with knowledge of these basic tools—you may well take additional courses where you will develop and adapt your skills further. That's not a problem—building on these skills with new approaches is how writing works, as each writing situation is different.

If you have a good grasp of these ideas, though, you will be able to adapt them fairly easily to additional writing situations, audiences, purposes, and formats. In other words, although each writing situation is different, the basic tools described here are portable.

Self-Check 2

Refer back to the first self-check at the beginning of this module. Have your ideas changed? What new ideas do you have? Write them out in the chart below.

Based on the objectives at the start, how have my views changed since the beginning of this module?	What new information do I have?

Activities

Before turning to the next module, check your understanding of the concepts and terms of this module by completing the activities below.

1. a) Go back to the sample paragraph that opens this module. Jot down notes, in your own words, about how it can be improved based on the advice given in the module. Write your notes in point form, but link them to specific words, phrases, and sentences in the paragraph. Try to write your notes without looking back at the module at first, but you can of course go back to refresh your memory if you need to do so.

   b) With a partner, use your notes to explain your observations to each other.

2. Consider the following topic sentences. Which ones effectively communicate an argument? Which ones do not? Why?

   a) Agnesi's proposal would not work.

   b) According to Agnesi, "students cannot calculate basic percentages."

   c) By basing her argument on an insulting overgeneralization about students, Agnesi demonstrates intellectually unethical behaviour.

   d) Agnesi wants all students to take math.

   e) Agnesi argues that all students should take math; however, she provides no evidence beyond potentially flawed examples based on her personal experiences.

3. The following paragraph has blanks indicating where transitions have been removed. Note the effect of these missing transitions on coherence and cohesion, and then add the missing transitions from the list on the next page. You will need to change capitalization in some cases to make the transitions fit. Note: if you have not already done so, you may wish to read Modules 2.1 and 2.2 (especially pages 174–179 of 2.2) before completing this activity.

   Zacarias' proposal for a mandatory "gap year" suffers from a lack of evidence _____ colleges and universities should not take her suggestions seriously. _____ Zacarias overly relies on hasty generalizations to support her point. _____ she claims that all eighteen-year-olds are "basically children" _____ they "lack proper time-management skills" and "aren't used to taking responsibility for their actions." _____ Zacarias' claims, not all students entering college or university fit into her absolute assumptions. Many students are very good at time management, and many other ones are very responsible. _____ Zacarias' only specific example is that of Prince William. Prince William is a particularly cherry-picked example _____ _____ almost no Canadian college or university students could relate to his life. _____ it is true that some students do experience stress when they first enroll in post-secondary education _____ colleges and universities should carefully research possible solutions to help students manage stress effectively.

, so	, so
, though,	despite
because	because
for example,	furthermore,
in her essay,	on the other hand,

4. a) You have a friend who is writing an essay and is having trouble with body paragraphs. How would you explain how the following paragraph illustrates concepts presented in this module? What is well done? What needs improvement? Write notes on what you would say in point form, but link your points to specific words, phrases, and sentences in the paragraph. Use the learning objectives at the beginning of this module and the checklist on page 111 at the end as a guide.

> According to Mae Agnesi, colleges should require that all students take math. Agnesi does not provide any discussion of how her proposal would work practically. Her proposal has practical problems because she does not consider how colleges would pay for these extra courses.

   b) In pairs, exchange explanations (verbally, not in writing) with your partner. Do you have the same points? What's different?

   c) Revise the paragraph above, paying particular attention to the Module 1.7 checklist. Also, use your notes from Activity 1. Compare your revisions with your partner's.

5. Select one of the effective topic sentences in Activity 2 and write the rest of the body paragraph that it has introduced.

6. Look at an essay that you have written and complete these steps:

   a) Look at your body paragraphs and consider how you have achieved cohesion among them. Underline all repeated keywords and transitions, and compare what you have done with the discussion of cohesion between paragraphs in this module.

   b) If your paragraphs don't connect as cohesively as they could, use the techniques from this module to improve cohesion. Consult Appendix B for a more complete list of transition words and phrases that you can use.

   c) Exchange your essay with a partner. Compare your approaches to cohesion with your partner's and discuss.

7. Your teacher will provide you with a published essay to evaluate how the writer has moved from one paragraph to another.

   a) Look at the body paragraphs that the author has written and consider how he or she has achieved cohesion from one paragraph to the next. Underline all repeated keywords and transitions, and compare our discussion of cohesion between paragraphs in this module with what the author has done.

   b) With a partner, exchange your notes on the published essay that you've examined. Compare your notes to make sure that you've noted all of the keyword repetitions and transitions. Discuss anything that one of you identified that the other person missed.

8. Your teacher will provide you with a text. Write body paragraphs for an essay in response to the text provided. Note that you will have to write an introduction first. If the text is the same one provided by your teacher in Module 1.6, you will have already written an effective introduction, so you may simply attach your new body paragraphs to it.

   Pay careful attention to this module's checklist on page 111 as you work. Also use your notes from Activity 1. Try to write fully developed body paragraphs because you will be asked to work on this example essay in other activities in this book.

How to Write Conclusions

[MODULE 1.8]

How to Write Conclusions

Module Objectives

Upon successful completion of this module, you will be able to

1. explain the importance of strong conclusions for effective writing

2. explain the relationship between conclusions and prior sections of essays

3. apply selected techniques (basic argument recap, keyword repetition, call for additional action) to the writing of effective conclusions

4. apply sentence-level techniques for controlling emphasis in conclusions

5. write conclusions to critical response essays

Self-Check 1

Read the module objectives above. You've probably encountered some of these terms and concepts before; others, however, will likely be new. In point form, identify what seems familiar and what seems new to you in the chart below.

What do I already know about the topics in this module's objectives?	What seems new to me?

Last Impressions

Do you ever get a second chance to make a *last* impression? That may sound like a strange question, mostly because we are used to hearing about *first* impressions. Just as people will make judgments about others within the first few minutes of meeting someone, we also will make judgments about someone based on the last things that they say before we go our separate ways.

You know that truly effective introductions capture attention and interest, and inspire trust and confidence—we focused on those in Module 1.6. Introductions can make a positive first impression, and your ability to write such introductions helps determine how persuasive or credible a reader finds you. The importance of *last* impressions also applies to writing—both the first words *and* the last words stick in your reader's memory, so you need to craft these carefully.

So we will now explore how to *conclude* our essay effectively. Successful conclusions help you to gain acceptance from your reader; a good conclusion will solidify a reader's cooperation or willingness to act as you have recommended. In essays, this "cooperation" will likely be the reader's agreement that you have made a fair and effective argument. In many workplace-related writing situations, a strong conclusion may help you to get a job you've applied for, a contract that your company has bid on, or an acceptance for a proposal that you've worked on.

Fortunately, as you've learned in the other modules, you don't need to come up with something completely new every time you write: there are standard techniques for writing conclusions, just as there are for introductions and body paragraphs. The following sections review these techniques, from simple to more complex.

What Does a Conclusion Do, Anyway?

In an essay, you are going to have some options when writing your conclusions. We need to survey the important features of a good conclusion. We've already noted that an effective conclusion leaves a lasting favourable impression on the reader. How does it do that, though?

There are a few expectations that a reader has about a conclusion in an argumentative essay. It should briefly summarize the thesis of your essay, and it should remind the readers of certain key points that you made. However, an effective conclusion may also suggest further study of a particular topic. For example, your short essay is not enough to say everything there is to say on an issue, but you might be able to help another writer develop these ideas further. A conclusion should close off your essay, but it could also open up a conversation. Lastly, a conclusion is a place where many writers try to use a memorable word or short phrase that will stick in the reader's mind. These closing sentences are the last thing that a reader will read, so they are often the first thing that he or she will remember.

Types of Conclusions

Tell Them What You Told Them: The Look-Back Conclusion

The simplest way to conclude a piece of writing is to use this formula:

In conclusion, + a restatement of your overall argument

Basically, this type of conclusion wraps things up by restating your overall argument more concisely. It reflects the last part of this old saying: "First, tell them what you're going to tell them. Next, tell them. Then, tell them what you told them."

look-back conclusion
A look-back conclusion reminds your reader of your main idea and some of the key points that you covered in your essay.

This is a simple, stripped-down approach that works best when you're in a hurry and don't have time to write something more complicated. The **look-back conclusion** does the most basic job of a conclusion in an essay: it reminds the reader of your main idea and some of the key points that you covered in your essay.

Here is an example of a look-back conclusion from Louise Zacarias' "Students Need a Gap Year":

> For these reasons, to make sure that all students are sufficiently mature and ready to meet the challenges of post-secondary education, colleges and universities should all require that students take at least a year off between the end of high school and the start of any additional schooling.

Zacarias' conclusion here reminds the reader of her thesis—that students should take "at least a year off" between high school and post-secondary studies. She also briefly recalls one of her main ideas: students are not currently mature enough to handle post-secondary studies right out of high school. She does all of this in one sentence, and she begins her conclusion with an alternative phrase that stands in for *In conclusion*. Remember from Module 1.5 (page 76) that you are free to begin your concluding paragraph with phrases other than *In conclusion*—phrases that do the same job of transitioning into your concluding thought.

Because an effective conclusion bookends an essay with an effective introduction, let's now imagine an introduction we have written in an essay responding to Zacarias' article.

Though there are many other ways of introducing this kind of essay response (as covered in Module 1.6), here we are using the two-part introduction covered on pages 86–87 where we summarize the original text and suggest a simple thesis statement that rejects Zacarias' claims:

> In "Students Need a Gap Year," Louise Zacarias contends that colleges and universities should "require that students take a 'gap year' before signing up for more school." According to Zacarias, "[e]ighteen-year-olds are basically children" because "they lack proper time-management skills, they haven't lived on their own before, and they aren't used to taking responsibility for their own actions." Thus, they need to become more mature before they start post-secondary education. She argues that a "gap year," a year off between high school and college/university, would provide students with greater maturity and solve these problems. Although Zacarias appears to mean well, her proposal has serious flaws: not only does she present an unsupported, insulting, hastily generalized argument, but she also ignores practical details. Moreover, her proposal is fundamentally unfair because it removes students' rights to make choices about their own studies. Thus, colleges and universities should not impose a gap year on students: students should retain the right to determine the timing of their own educations.

If we wanted to write a short look-back conclusion to this introduction, we might say the following:

> In short, Zacarias' claims are filled with cherry-picked examples and sweeping generalizations. Her proposal is unworkable and unethical, and thus students should not be required to take a year off between high school and college or university.

Again, the conclusion here restates the thesis and the main points that you've made throughout the rest of your essay, and it does so in two short sentences.

However, the look-back conclusion has one basic flaw: it can be boring. It does the bare minimum of what you'd expect a conclusion to do, but it doesn't really leave the reader with a particularly positive last impression. The look-back conclusion may be efficient, but there is nothing attention-grabbing about it. In fact, essays with conclusions that begin "In conclusion" and then briefly restate the introduction are really common, so your essay—if it does exactly the same thing—will not stand out in a positive way. With a little more time (and it doesn't take that long), you can push your conclusions much further.

What Next?: The Look-Ahead Conclusion

The look-ahead conclusion strategy uses the argument that you've made so far as a jumping-off point into something new. You may have heard that you shouldn't introduce new material in your conclusion. Although this advice is generally good, it requires further explanation.

The *actual* advice that you should follow is that you should not introduce new lines of unsupported argumentation in your conclusion. Argumentative statements without sufficient explanation are often going to be unsupported generalizations, and using those in your conclusion will not leave a favourable impression on a critical reader of your essay.

However, it's really important not to confuse the idea that you should not introduce new, unsupported claims in your conclusion with the idea that you *can* introduce new approaches that your reader can and should take. For example, your conclusion can point out new directions based on your argument.

look-ahead conclusion
A look-ahead conclusion suggests further directions that your argument might take.

The easiest version of the **look-ahead conclusion** might point out any of the following things:

- the reader should do more research regarding the topic
- the reader should carry out your thesis following a set proposal or plan
- the reader should carry out the alternatives to the original writer's claims that you've suggested earlier in the essay

You might also combine two or three of these features into the same conclusion—it depends on what you're writing about, your audience, and how much time you have, among other things.

In the case of our response to Louise Zacarias' article, we have seen what a look-back conclusion would look like. Here is a possible look-ahead conclusion:

> In retrospect, Louise Zacarias' argument does leave some unanswered questions. Perhaps many students coming out of high school and going directly into post-secondary studies are experiencing an overly difficult transition. Failure in post-secondary studies is costly, and the government and the schools ought to work together to study the pressures that new students face to see if the problem is truly as widespread as Zacarias believes. If the problem is indeed severe, schools need to provide some additional resources to new students to help make the transition to post-secondary school less stressful.

You'll notice immediately that this conclusion is longer. A look-ahead conclusion is more difficult to write in just one or two short sentences because you are suggesting that your readers take some kind of action (do more research/study, follow a new plan), and that suggestion takes time to express clearly.

You'll also notice that this conclusion doesn't really address what the writer said earlier in the essay. There's little doubt that this writer has spent some time discussing the problems with Zacarias' claims that all students are immature, but that fact is only hinted at here when the writer suggests that the study will find out if this problem is truly "widespread" or "severe." Nothing is mentioned here about this ethical argument: students should be allowed to determine when they attend post-secondary school.

If you don't clearly address your thesis and key points in your conclusion, your essay may be seen as somewhat weak in the end; thus, the look-ahead conclusion has its own drawbacks. However, this kind of conclusion will help your essay to stand out because it isn't as predictable as the look-back conclusion. In addition, the look-ahead conclusion could really clinch your argument as a whole, and your suggestion for further action on the part of your reader may just be the key to leaving a favourable last impression.

The Combo: The Look-Both-Ways Conclusion

As you've learned, you can almost always combine writing techniques, and conclusions are no exception. Sometimes the most effective conclusions look backward—reminding the reader of what you've said in your earlier paragraphs—*and* look forward, emphasizing what should happen next with regard to the issue under discussion.

We might end our critical response to Zacarias' argument a third way, with the following combo conclusion:

> Zacarias' argument fails because of serious evidentiary, practical, and ethical problems. Certainly students may choose to take a "gap year" if they wish; however, colleges and universities should not force them to do so. Despite the problems with her argument, however, Zacarias does have one good point: she is right that some (though not all) students need help with the transition from high school to college or university. To help such students, colleges and universities should research ways of working with both students and their parents to help them develop their skills, maturity, and independence. Such programs could help solve the problems that Zacarias discusses, but students should be the ones to decide whether they need them. After all, the point of education is to give people more choices—not take them away.

One thing we should note immediately is this conclusion's strong link to the essay's introduction. Even though we haven't used the phrase *In conclusion*, or anything even similar to that phrase, the conclusion clearly reflects on the main points of our argument, which signals to the reader that we are wrapping up our essay. However, you should check with your teacher about whether or not you should use a phrase like *In conclusion*—or something similar—because many readers do find a familiar phrase that opens the concluding paragraph of a short argumentative essay to be useful.

In addition, like our look-back conclusion earlier, this concluding paragraph completes a circle: it returns the reader to where he or she started, and ends the essay where it began. However—unlike the look-back conclusion we wrote above—this conclusion does not stop there. It also performs the main task of the look-ahead conclusion. It introduces so-called new material, but it does so in a focused way by suggesting that schools could study the issue further to determine new strategies to help students who opt to use these resources.

The **combo** or **look-both-ways conclusion**, as the name implies, combines the things that worked best about the other two types of conclusions: it reminds the reader of what you said before, and it proposes an interesting new direction to potentially explore. While these conclusions are longer, and take much more time to write, they are worth the effort because they stand out from an essay that just summarizes the argument in similar words (or from an essay that doesn't have a conclusion at all!).

> combo or look-both-ways conclusion
> The look-both-ways conclusion combines a review of your thesis and supporting evidence with suggestions for further directions that your argument might take.

Famous Last Words

The last sentence of the combo conclusion above is a direct and forceful appeal to the reader:

> After all, the point of education is to give people more choices—not take them away.

Why do you think the essay ends this way? We've already noted that a favourable last impression can be achieved by reminding the reader of your best arguments and suggesting alternative solutions to combat a problem. Moreover, you have an opportunity in the conclusion to express your position with some emotional force. When making arguments for your positions in essays, you will commonly restrain overly emotional language until the conclusion. Your audience is often diverse and may contain readers who disagree with your position, perhaps strongly.

Your best and safest approach to such an audience is often reason and objectivity. Those who already agree with your position will not likely be put off by reasoned and emotionally restrained supporting arguments; those who do not agree with you may be put off by any presentation that is not well reasoned. Strong emotional assertions or claims in support of something are usually only welcomed by readers who already agree with you.

For readers who disagree, your best hope is to demonstrate reason and fairness by deliberately restraining strong emotion. By the time you arrive at your conclusion, you will have done your best to achieve a reasoned and rational presentation in a balanced and deliberate way.

Remember that you have already employed the techniques we covered in Module 1.7 to write detailed and well-supported body paragraphs. Now, you have earned the right to some emotion, and if your arguments have been effective with your audience, a short emotional appeal at the end of your conclusion might tip the balance in your favour.

In the last sentence of the combo conclusion above, the writer has tried to make a direct address to the readers to remind them of the importance of choice in education. This argument has been central to the writer's claims that Zacarias completely overrides the students' wishes in her proposal.

clincher
A clincher is the final sentence of your essay. A good clincher will leave a memorable impression on the reader.

This final sentence is sometimes called the **clincher** sentence. If some emotional force has been earned and is appropriate in the conclusion, a little drama is also earned, appropriate, and effective in the closing sentence. Because this clincher is the final impression you will leave on a reader, you want to ensure that it is as memorable as possible.

It is often effective for this final sentence to contain several short, even single-syllable, words and to use punctuation like dashes (see also Module 2.2). The writer of our conclusion has taken both of these suggestions in his or her essay, writing the words "—not take them away."

There are many famous examples of concluding "clincher" sentences. Just prior to the American Revolution, Patrick Henry was reported to have concluded a speech with the following line:

> Give me liberty, or give me death!

You should notice that Henry has used an emotional phrase, complete with short memorable words and an exclamation point. The line was recalled by almost everyone who attended the event, even though his speech was not written down until much later. We don't recommend using exclamation points very often in a formal essay; however, if there is one place in an essay where such a piece of punctuation *may be* appropriate, it is in the clincher.

Politicians understand very well the power of a memorable closing line. Just prior to the 1995 Quebec referendum on sovereignty, Prime Minister Jean Chrétien made a speech in which he appealed for national unity. He concluded with the following lines:

> In a few days, all the shouting will be over. And at that moment, you will be alone to make your decision. At that moment I urge you, my fellow Quebecers, to listen to your heart—and to your head.
>
> I am confident that Quebec and Canada will emerge strong and united.
>
> Thank you. And good night.

The words here are emotionally charged and quite short. The prime minister has even paused with a dash for greater effect.

You do not have to create historically enduring sentences like these in your writing, but you should try to create a final sentence that is forceful and memorable, a sentence that may be just the emotional push a reader needs to fully agree with your whole essay.

Module Checklist

In my conclusion, have I

- ☐ provided my reader with a brief recap of the key points that I made in the body of my essay?
- ☐ suggested to the reader some kind of further action that can be taken (more research, an alternative solution, etc.)?
- ☐ made sure that any new material that I introduce is not an unsupported generalization?
- ☐ ended with some kind of memorable clinching thought that leaves an impression on my reader?

Looking Ahead

The goal of this module was to explain that last—and first—impressions are equally important in effective writing. A good conclusion that has been supported all along by careful reasons and arguments will help you to achieve your goal of persuading your reader to agree with your overall argument.

Many of the strategies for successful conclusions in critical response essays work very well in other kinds of writing too. An argumentative research essay will have used a number of secondary sources to build up its claims, so readers will need even more last-minute guidance to help them interpret the material.

In addition, many kinds of workplace writing attempt to convince someone to do something. For example, a good cover letter should make a positive last impression on your potential employer. That last impression will make it far more likely that you'll be offered an interview. A proposal that ends with a clear and concise indication of what should be done is more likely to be accepted.

Conclusions are an important component in writing persuasively, and much of the writing that you will do in school and afterward will be geared toward persuading your reader to do something or to think a certain way.

Self-Check 2

Refer back to the first self-check at the beginning of this module. Have your ideas changed? What new ideas do you have? Write them out in the chart below.

Based on the objectives at the start, how have my views changed since the beginning of this module?	What new information do I have?

Activities

Before turning to the next module, check your understanding of the concepts and terms of this module by completing the activities below.

1. Based on your understanding of the different types of conclusions covered in this module, fill in the table below with one strength and one weakness for each type:

	Look-back conclusion	Look-ahead conclusion	Combo conclusion
Strengths			
Weaknesses			

2. Your friend has asked you to proofread an essay she has written in response to an article that suggests that we should ban all cars that are not fully electric. She has written the following conclusion:

   > In conclusion, we shouldn't listen to the author. His ideas about banning any non-electric cars won't work. Plus, I like driving my Escalade. We shouldn't listen to him.

   Based on the information covered in this module, what would you say to her about her work? Start by making a list of both what works well and what the drawbacks are, and then suggest how the conclusion could be made more effective.

3. In pairs, discuss your observations about good conclusions using the notes that you made in Activity 2. Make note of anything different your partner may have suggested that seems valid and could be added to your notes. You will then have a quick reference sheet to assist you in writing improved conclusions.

4. Read the following clincher sentences written in response to Louise Zacarias' "Students Need a Gap Year." Suggest what might be done to improve each one. Is one particularly effective? If you think so, note why.

    a) In the end, we shouldn't do what she says.

    b) Louise Zacarias makes many interesting claims, but her general idea that students must take a year off between high school and post-secondary studies cannot be supported.

    c) The only solution is obvious: students must be allowed to make their own decisions about their futures.

    d) Don't you think that students should get to decide when they get to go to college or university?

    e) In conclusion, the author is wrong.

5. In Module 1.7 on pages 106–108, we looked at two body paragraphs that were a response to Mae Agnesi's article "The Future = Math Required." Look at the conclusion to this response below. Its sentences are scrambled. Rewrite the conclusion, putting the sentences into the correct order.

> She does not differentiate between students who have different ability levels. In fact, she relies so much on sweeping generalizations and cherry-picked examples that there may not actually be a problem at all. To summarize, Mae Agnesi's argument that all students should be required to take math courses at college is unworkable and unsupported. As with most situations, a one-size-fits-all solution actually fits no one. Post-secondary institutions should study the situation carefully. If they determine that their graduates are not getting jobs because of math deficiencies, then they should work to improve the math skills of students who need the extra help. Furthermore, she never indicates how colleges are supposed to pay for these courses.

6. In the Activities section in Modules 1.6 and 1.7, you were asked to write a model essay responding to a new article that your teacher had given to you. Now it is time to write its conclusion. Try to write a fully developed conclusion because you will be asked to work on this example essay in other activities in this book.

    a) Remember that there are times, including some exam situations, when you will be asked to write a timed essay, so you need to be able to write a conclusion quickly. Write a basic look-back conclusion to your essay from Module 1.7. Try to write the conclusion to your essay quickly, but make sure that you are still writing a complete look-back conclusion. Your teacher may wish to actually assign this activity as a timed exercise in your class.

b) There are also times when you will be given more out-of-class time to write your essays. This extra time will allow you to revise your conclusions. Expand the look-back conclusion you wrote for 6 (a) above to make it into a combo conclusion. Use the Module Checklist and the reference sheet that you made with your partner in Activities 2 and 3 to help you to make the conclusion as complete and memorable as possible.

Is This on the Test? Writing Essay Exams

[MODULE **1.9**]

Is This on the Test? Writing Essay Exams

Module Objectives

Upon successful completion of this module, you will be able to

1. use organizational strategies to prepare for essay exams
2. develop a personal, course-by-course plan for dealing with essay exams
3. adapt advice given earlier in this book to essay exams

Self-Check 1

Read the module objectives above. You've probably encountered some of these terms and concepts before; others, however, will likely be new. In point form, identify what seems familiar and what seems new to you in the chart below.

What do I already know about the topics in this module's objectives?	What seems new to me?

Essay Exams: Don't Just Walk In

Think about exams that you've written in the past. Did you ever feel particularly good about a certain answer you wrote? What do you think contributed to that good experience? Have you ever turned to the long-answer or essay questions on a test and felt that there were certain questions you were well prepared for? Alternatively, have you ever had problems with essay exams? What could you have done differently?

As we discussed in Module 1.5, many courses that have out-of-class essays also have in-class essay tests and exams. To keep things simple, we'll just use the term *exams* from now on to refer to both tests and exams.

Students often need help with writing essay exams. Essay exams can be especially challenging because there isn't always time to reflect on or revise what you write before handing it in. Despite this challenge, however, you can prepare for essay exams, and this module tells you how.

Actually, you can take the skills we've covered so far in this book and put them to work immediately in any college course that requires an essay exam. This module offers general advice for getting ready to write exams as well as specific advice about what and how to write.

Although we present tried-and-true advice here, keep in mind that your best resource for information about exams in a particular course is the teacher for that course—always ask if you have questions. This module will help you know what kinds of questions to ask.

Right from the Start: Reading Your Course Outline

Preparation for exams doesn't start the week or day or night before. It actually starts on the first day of class. You probably don't have time to stay right up to the minute in all your courses all the time, but gradual work throughout a course beats caffeine-powered all-nighters every time. Thus, the first section of this module doesn't start with the exam. Instead, it starts with the first day of class.

The first thing you can find out is whether your courses have exams—some probably do, and some probably don't. If they do, do they involve essay writing? Courses in history, philosophy, and English literature tend to have essay exams. Other areas—such as anthropology, psychology, sociology, political science, and business—can vary. Sometimes exams will be 100 per cent essay based; other times they will have a mixture.

Check your course outline or syllabus at the beginning of the semester. It will tell you whether there is an exam, how much of your grade percentage it's worth, whether it's in the last week of classes or during the exam period, and similar vital information. Most importantly, be sure to check all the dates!

As the Course Goes On

During the course, you will want to take careful notes about the class content. Exam preparation occurs throughout the semester, not just in the hours before your final test! Not only should you focus on the key concepts that are discussed in class, but you should also make note of how the course is structured and evaluated.

There may be times when the teacher refers to how he or she designs exam questions—you should make special note of such moments. Record them in your notes in such a way so that you can easily find them later.

In particular, pay close to attention to the answers to these questions:

- What material did your teacher talk about the most?
- Did he or she give any hints about the exam?
- Did he or she post any instructions about the format of the exam and the types of questions?

As a general rule, whatever your teacher spends the most time on in class will probably be worth the most marks on the exam. In terms of course content, take special note of

- terms/definitions
- applications of terms and definitions
- explanations of theories/approaches
- applications of these theories/approaches to situations

These are common course elements that often show up in essay questions on exams.

When in doubt, ask your teacher. However, don't ask, "Is this on the test?" Teachers generally dislike this question.

It might be better to ask your teacher if he or she has time to do a tutorial on how to answer exam questions. You might also ask if there are any particular recommendations about how/what to study for the exam.

When the Exam Schedule Comes Out

Tests and exams scheduled during class time will usually be specified in the course outline. Final exams, on the other hand, appear in the exam schedule, which generally isn't available until later in the semester. All of this can vary depending on your school, so make sure you know how exams are scheduled at your school.

As with your course outlines, when the exam schedule comes out, check all your courses and figure out when and where the exams are held—take note of the dates, times, and locations.

Once you've looked over your exam schedule, make sure you know the answer to each of the following questions:

- Do you have any conflicts?
- Do you have several exams on the same day, or in tight clusters?
- Do you need to make sure that you book time off from work to avoid conflicts with the exams?

Knowing when your exams are and how they are scheduled in relation to each other will help you plan. If you have two exams at the same time or several exams in the same 24-hour period, you should talk to your teacher about what to do in the case of exam conflicts.

A few weeks before the actual exams, you should double-check the dates and times to make sure you have not misread the schedule.

What to Bring to the Exam

At minimum, you need to bring a pen or a pencil to the exam. Here is a tip: unless your teacher has specifically asked you to write in pencil, *write in either blue or black pen*. Pencil can be very difficult for the teacher to read.

For some exams, teachers allow students to bring notes, various reference materials, or even the textbook. Such "open-book" exams aren't actually as easy as they sound, as teachers usually mark them harder, but if you do have an open-book exam, make sure that you bring everything you are allowed to have. Also, make sure that your notes are well organized. You want to spend most of your time writing, not searching through disorganized materials trying to find what you are looking for.

Here's another important tip: know the material, even for open-book exams. Open-book exams are tricky because unprepared students think they can look up everything during the exam, and then they run out of time.

During the Exam

Read the Instructions!

Your teachers have usually spent a long time writing the instructions for your exam, so make sure you read them carefully. In the pressure of exam situations, however, many students glance at these instructions very briefly, and in some cases, skip them completely.

> Ignoring the instructions virtually guarantees that you will get a low mark on the exam!

Pay particular attention to instructions about

- how many questions to answer
- how many readings to discuss in each question or in total
- any restrictions on how you can answer a question
- how much time to spend on each question
- how many marks are associated with each question

Budget Your Time

You need to know exactly how long the exam is, and you should plan out how long you should spend on each section/question. For example, if the exam is three hours (180 minutes) long, and a section is worth 10 per cent of the total marks, you should spend approximately 10 per cent of your time on this question (18 minutes, give or take). Whatever you do, don't spend too much time on sections worth too few marks!

In some cases, your teachers may have actually given you suggested guidelines for how long to spend on each section of an exam. These guidelines frequently reflect the marks breakdown of the exam, and they almost always appear in the instructions. These helpful suggestions are yet another reason why you should read and follow the instructions carefully!

Specific Advice about Types of Questions

The hardest part of an exam is when you're sitting in the room, quiet at your desk, with the paper in front of you, staring at the questions themselves. Unlike many other writing situations, in which you can consult references, including this book, while writing, essay exams usually don't allow for such consultation.

As we've said, preparing for such exams really begins on the first day of class. Nevertheless, there are certain patterns in exam questions, and if you are aware of these patterns, you'll be better able to do well with your responses. In this section, we'll take a look at the typical instructions and keywords used on essay exams.

Your first goal is to read the exam questions carefully. Look for keywords. Questions will often name concepts, theories, or terms from the course and then ask you to do something with this information. We'll expand on each of the following types of exam questions in more detail later in the module.

If you have an exam with any of these kinds of questions, ask your teacher for more information about how you should approach them.

Types of Essay Questions on Exams

- analyze a passage/quotation
- explain a concept, define a term, and apply your explanation or definition
- discuss a given statement
- compare two or more texts, aspects, or details covered in the course content

Watch out in particular for these question keywords:

- define/definition
- describe/description
- summarize/summary
- explain/explanation
- analyze/analysis
- compare/contrast
- apply/application
- critical/critique/critically respond

Analyze a Passage/Quotation

A passage or quotation analysis question will usually ask you to read a (relatively) short text that you likely haven't seen before. You will need to apply key concepts from the course to the passage that you have been given.

For example, in an exam for an English literature class, you might be given a paragraph or two from an essay, short story, or novel, or you might be required to read an entire short poem. To write a successful answer, you need to read the passage closely and focus on any key features that relate to the larger themes of the course.

Sometimes, you are just given a short quotation, which is designed to get you to think about a key concept from the course. Unless your teacher asks you to do so, don't write out the entire quotation in the exam book. You don't get marks for copying words from one piece of paper to another, and it wastes time that you could spend writing your answer—which you do get marks for.

In both passage and quotation analysis exam questions, you should generally follow the advice from the rest of this book: use signal phrases to introduce key details (Module 1.3), craft a thesis about these key details (Module 1.6), and so on. Because it's the fastest way to reference a text, you should probably focus on using short, relevant quotations from the passage in your answer.

Explain a Concept or Define a Term

It is extremely common to see essay-exam questions that ask you to define a term or explain a key concept from the course. Teachers see these questions as particularly useful measures of how well you've understood the course content.

For example, in a religion class, you might be asked to define the term *transubstantiation* and use it to identify important differences between Roman Catholicism and Protestantism. In order to successfully answer that question, you would need to know both the definition of the term and also the key concepts of the doctrine that your teacher would have covered in class.

If a teacher asks you to define a term and discuss its importance, he or she has actually helped to set up the structure of your response for you. Many students find the introduction a particularly difficult thing to write in a time-sensitive exam setting because they don't know where to begin. However, if you've been asked to define a key term or concept, your teacher has given you a hint on where you should begin: provide as clear and accurate a definition of the key term as possible.

Once you have defined the term or concept, you can use your thesis statement to indicate how you will *apply* the term or concept to the course content. Explaining the relationship of the concepts to subjects studied in the class will thus make up the body paragraphs of your response.

Discuss a Given Statement

A teacher may provide you with a provocative statement about an issue covered in the course, and you are expected to respond to it. The structure of this type of exam question is very similar to what we've seen above with a quotation analysis. Sometimes the statement will be attributed to a critic and be in quotation marks, and sometimes it will just appear on its own. For example, you might see a question like the following:

> Nicholas Carr argues, "*For me, as for others, the Net is becoming a universal medium, the conduit for most of the information that flows through my eyes and ears and into my mind.*" Discuss the role that technology has played in accessing information in the Internet age.

Your response will work very much like a passage analysis. Examine the key ideas presented in the quotation and critically analyze the passage using the approaches covered in Module 1.4. Remember that critical analysis involves breaking down complex ideas into simpler, easier-to-manage elements. Look at the statement you are given, relate it to a key concept from the course, and start writing your answer. Regardless of which position you take, be sure to provide relevant supporting evidence from the course.

Compare and Contrast Two or More Ideas

Sometimes an exam question will ask you to look at two (or more) texts that are related to each other because of a similar plot, structure, key thematic concern, or idea that was discussed by your teacher in class.

Alternatively, you might be asked to look at two different viewpoints on a similar issue. For example, imagine you were asked to compare and contrast the king of the gods in Greek and Norse mythology. Your responsibility would be to find the similarities and differences between Zeus and Odin, and you'd need to supply as evidence whatever class material was relevant to those claims.

To successfully answer a compare-and-contrast exam question, you should spend the same amount of time joining the two ideas together as you do splitting them apart. You'll want to be very clear about how you are going to approach the answer to the question. The introduction, as with a definition question, will be a good place to clearly establish your terms.

Once you've established the framework of your answer, you should try to establish the common ground in your comparison part of the essay, and then you should clearly delineate the key differences (and *why* you think they are different) in the contrast section of your response.

How to Handle Question Keywords

You will encounter many of the keywords in the following chart on exam questions, often in combination with other words. Keywords will help you to determine which type of question you are being asked, but don't be surprised to see questions that overlap rows of this table.

Where appropriate, the table includes references to other sections of this book that can be used to improve your ability to successfully answer essay-exam questions.

Key term	What you should know
define/ definition	The question may specifically ask you to define terms or concepts, but even if it doesn't, you should define any term that you introduce into your answer, as your teacher will usually be looking for evidence that you understand the term.
	Also, defining a term/concept will help you apply it because your definition will set up what comes next.
describe/ description	Words like *describe* and *explain* are also common. For example, if you are asked to "describe, explain, and apply" a concept, you might first define the concept briefly, then provide a more detailed overview of the concept.
	You would then apply all of this to a specific situation or example. In such cases, transitions like *for example* will be especially useful to you, resulting in sentences like this one: For example, _____ relates to _____ in the following way: _____ [explanation].
summarize/ summary	Module 1.3 specifically addresses how to summarize a text. Even if you're not specifically directed to summarize something in an exam question's instructions, you will have to use summary skills to define, describe, and analyze a passage/quotation.
analyze/ analysis	Analysis, as any dictionary will tell you, involves breaking things into pieces and explaining how the pieces fit together.
	Take a look at Module 1.4 to refresh your memory about how to analyze texts, and note any suggestions that you think would help you to answer analysis questions on essay exams.

(Continued)

Key term	What you should know
explain/ explanation	Explanation usually involves analysis, as illustrated by the fact that it's difficult to do one without the other. If you're explaining a concept or theory, you will need to analyze how various terms, definitions, and sub-definitions all work together.

Pay careful attention to how your teacher introduces and explains key terms in class: if you try to model the same approach, you will be well prepared for the exam. |
| compare/ contrast | The instruction to "compare/contrast" relates specifically to material covered in Modules 1.6, 1.7, 2.1, and 2.2. In particular, the words *although*, *however*, and *but* are especially helpful for presenting similarities and differences between different terms, topics, concepts, and so on. |
| apply/ application | An exam question that asks you to apply a term, theory, or concept will require you to have a clear understanding of the term you are asked to apply. You need to demonstrate that you understand the term or theory that you are working with first, and then you need to use it to *explain* another text or idea.

You may need to quote from a passage that has been provided in the exam, so you should use the textual referencing skills from Module 1.3 to show the teacher that you understand the concept being tested. |
| critical/ critique/ critically respond | Most of Part 1—and Module 1.4 in particular—develops critical response skills. Remember that critically responding to a text requires you to assess the validity of its claims and to test them out using evidence.

Essay-exam questions will often require you to use critical thinking skills to fully answer them. However, you should also be aware that different subjects/fields handle critical thinking differently. Be sure to demonstrate the type of critical reasoning appropriate for the field of study. |

Again, this advice is general; remember that some terms within the chart will overlap with other terms. Please check with your individual subject teachers for more specific advice about the types of essay-exam questions in your individual courses and how each course's particular material will be tested at the final exam.

Answer the Questions in the Order That Works for You

The questions appear in a certain order; however, unless there are restrictions (such as an exam where Part I is collected before you can begin Part II), you are free to decide what you should do first. Check with your teacher if you're not sure, but, in general, the order of your answers doesn't matter so long as you clearly label them.

For example, suppose you're writing an essay exam in an English course with the following section weightings:

Section 1: 25 per cent

Section 2: 25 per cent

Section 3: 50 per cent

In this situation, you might choose to do Section 3 first, as it's worth the greatest number of marks.

Again, don't forget to clearly label the questions—this will make it easier for your teacher to grade!

Make Smart Choices

Sometimes exams have restrictions on the number of readings you can use in any one question. For example, many literature exams don't allow students to write about a particular text more than once.

Like most students, you probably know some texts better than others. Given this fact, you might make the smart choice to use the texts that you know best in the sections worth the most marks, when possible.

Module Checklist

Most other modules in this book provide you with a checklist that you can use to ensure you are applying all of the key concepts to an essay you might have been assigned to write.

In this module, we have a more general checklist that we recommend you use for each of your classes to help you to prepare for final exams.

- ☐ Are there tests/exams in this class?
- ☐ When are they? Check the course outline (and exam schedule when available). What are the exact dates and times?
- ☐ Have I double-checked this information and made sure that there are no conflicts (with work, planned trips, etc.)?
- ☐ How much is each test and exam worth?
- ☐ Are the tests/exams essay format, non-essay format, or a combination?
- ☐ What kinds of questions will be on the exam?
  - • Will I be asked to define terms, explain theories, apply terms/ theories to situations, analyze passages, critically respond to readings, etc.?
  - • Do I have examples in my notes and readings of all types of writing I will have to do on the exam?
  - • How does all of this relate to the topics/readings on my course outline?
- ☐ Will I have a choice of questions? How much choice?
- ☐ Are there any rules/restrictions that I need to know about?
- ☐ If I am entitled to accommodation according to my school's policies, have I made arrangements for these accommodations?
- ☐ If the test/exam is "open book," have I carefully read and understood what I'm allowed to bring into the exam? Have I carefully organized this material so that I can find what I need quickly during the exam?
- ☐ Do I have any questions about the exam and how to answer the questions? Can I ask my teacher? Can I visit the school's writing centre/learning centre?

Looking Ahead

The most immediate application for essay-exam skills, obviously, is in courses in college or university—for several years, you will have to take exams regularly, and many of these exams will require that you write essays.

Down the road, though, your exam-taking days may not be over. Some professional certification and licensing exams, for example, may require essays, and even if they don't, you will still find that some of the skills in this module apply.

Finally, more and more people are returning to college and university to obtain additional qualifications after they first graduate. You've probably heard that today's workplaces increasingly value life-long learning, and sometimes this learning involves going back to school to do another certificate, diploma, or degree later in life. In fact, it's becoming increasingly common for people in their 30s, 40s, and beyond to sign up for more courses.

All of this means that exam skills in general and essay-exam skills in particular are and will remain important to you.

Self-Check 2

Refer back to the first self-check at the beginning of this module. Have your ideas changed? What new ideas do you have? Write them out in the chart below.

Based on the objectives at the start, how have my views changed since the beginning of this module?	What new information do I have?

Activities

Before turning to the next module, check your understanding of the concepts and terms of this module by completing the activities below.

1. Think back to exams you have written in the past. Did you follow any of the advice from this chapter? If you answered "yes," what particular strategies did you use that helped you? If you answered "no," what specific piece of advice would you apply to future exams to help improve your exam answers?

2. Exchange the information from Activity 1 with a partner. Discuss.

3. For all your courses, check online to see if your teachers have posted any information about final exams. Do any of these exams involve essays? If yes, is there any information about the format? If no, ask your teachers.

4. When you have information about your exams, make a list of the ways in which advice given in this module may apply to these particular exams.

5. Apply the exam checklist at the end of the module to each one of your courses.

6. If possible, ask a teacher of one of your other courses if he or she can provide examples of the kinds of questions that will be on the exam. Try to write sample answers to those practice exam questions to see if you've understood the concepts being tested. Ask your teacher if he or she is willing to give you advice on how to improve your answer.

Grammar, Mechanics, and Style

What Is a Sentence?

[M O D U L E **2.1**]

What Is a Sentence?

Module Objectives

Upon successful completion of this module, you will be able to

1. define the term *sentence*

2. define the terms *verb* and *subject*

3. recognize verbs, subjects, and subordinating and coordinating conjunctions

4. define the terms *phrase* and *clause*

5. distinguish between phrases and clauses

6. recognize independent and subordinate clauses

7. recognize complete sentences

8. recognize a type of grammatical error called a sentence fragment

9. describe the importance of this module to the rest of this book

Self-Check 1

Read the module objectives above. You've probably encountered some of these terms and concepts before; others, however, will likely be new. In point form, identify what seems familiar and what seems new to you in the chart below.

What do I already know about the topics in this module's objectives?	What seems new to me?

What Is a Sentence, Anyway?

Some of the following word groups are sentences, and some are not:

1. Students should have to take a year off between high school and college/university.
2. According to Zacarias.
3. Because students aren't mature enough to attend college/university right away.
4. In order to become more mature.
5. They need an extra year of personal growth.

Which ones aren't sentences?

If you determined that (1) and (5) are sentences and that (2), (3), and (4) are not sentences, you're right. If so, good! If not, by the end of this module, you will definitely know the right answers.

Here's another question: if you were right about the sentences and non-sentences above, consider these questions:

- Do you know why you were right?
- How would you explain your reasoning to someone else?

This module is all about the answers to these questions.

Skilled workers need to understand their tools. For writers, these tools are sentences. We use sentences every day: when we talk to someone, or write an email or a text, we're often creating sentences. When we talk to someone, though, we can stop and repeat ourselves if the person needs an explanation. Doing so is really easy because speaking is fast and easy: we've been doing it since we were a few years old.

Writing, however, is more difficult. If the person you are writing to doesn't understand your message, he or she has to write a question and send it to you. Then you have to read it, write the answer, and so on—back and forth, back and forth.

Poorly written, confusing, or incomplete sentences in these situations can make the process of understanding them seem like it takes forever. It saves time and effort to write sentences properly in the first place.

An incomplete sentence is merely a group of words disguised as a sentence, starting with a capital letter and ending with a period. In general, the term *fragment* refers to an incomplete part of something larger, so we call these incomplete parts of sentences **sentence fragments**.

What, then, makes a complete sentence, as opposed to a sentence fragment? Let's look at some possible definitions.

Which of the following definitions of the term *sentence* have you heard before?

1. A sentence is a complete thought (or a complete idea).
2. A sentence starts with a capital letter and ends with a period.
3. A sentence has a verb and a subject.

The problem with (1) is that in order to apply this definition, you have to define *thought* or *idea*, and these terms are really difficult to define. (2) doesn't work at all. I could type this:

The.

According to (2), the above example would be a sentence. Clearly it's not, and any definition that gives you the wrong answer isn't very useful.

You may be thinking that (3) sounds right. If so, you're on the right track: in fact, any sentence does have to have a verb and a subject. The problem with (3) is that it's missing an additional piece of information.

However, it's a start, and we're actually going to begin explaining what a sentence is by discussing the two terms in this definition: verbs and subjects.

Verbs

The first rule of sentences is that they have to have verbs: without a verb, you don't have a sentence. You may have a group of words on a page, but if it's verbless, it's not technically a sentence. Consider the following word groups:

1. A bright red t-shirt.
2. My brother's wife and her young daughter.
3. My brother's wife and her young daughter both wore bright red t-shirts.

Which one of these groups of words is a sentence? You have probably guessed (3), but why?

---

sentence fragment
A sentence fragment is a group of words that is disguised as a sentence but is incomplete.

(1) makes no sense. "A bright red t-shirt" *what*? Does someone have it? Is something happening with it? Who has it? Who is doing something with it? (1) doesn't say. It's not a sentence.

(2) has the same problem. Are these people somewhere? Are they doing something? We don't know because there are no additional words there to tell us.

(3) solves the mysteries of (1) and (2) by joining together the two groups of words with *wore*, thus completing the relationship.

The word *wore*, of course, is a verb—the past tense of the verb *wear*. Wearing the t-shirts is what the wife and the daughter are doing, so the **verb** describes an action or a state (you can think of it in both senses). The verb here completes the relationship between the people doing the wearing and the t-shirts.

> **verb**
> A verb is a word that indicates actions, states/conditions, or feelings.

As we just suggested, verbs don't always indicate actions. Sometimes they also indicate states/conditions or feelings, as in these examples:

- I am cold.
- He seems upset.
- They have a new car.
- She feels confident.

None of the verbs in the sentences above describe what someone (or something) is doing. Instead, these verbs describe states: the state/condition of being cold, the state/condition of seeming upset, the state/condition of having (in the sense of possessing) a new car, and the state/condition of feeling confident.

A verb is thus the most basic element of a sentence: without a verb, you might have a group of words, and the group might even start with a capital letter and end with a period, but—despite this sentence-like formatting—without a verb, it's still not a sentence.

We use verbs every day to describe what we're saying and doing, and what we're feeling and being. In certain types of communication, we tend to use verbs to express more abstract concepts. Examples include words like *argues*, *claims*, and some of the other signal-phrase verbs from Module 1.3.

In other words, verbs turn up whenever anyone says or writes anything, and that's why it's so important to understand how they work.

helping verbs
Helping verbs do not
appear on their own,
so they must team up
with a main verb to
have meaning. Some
verbs can be both
helping verbs and main
verbs.

Some verbs, called **helping verbs**, do not appear on their own: in order to have meaning, they must team up with a main verb. Examples of helping verbs include

should, could, would, may, might, must, will, do, be (is, are, was, were, will be, have been), have (and its various forms).

Yes, you might be thinking that we sometimes do use these words on their own, as in this example:

Are you studying tonight?

Well, I should.

As we pointed out in Module 1.2, speaking and writing are different. You can get away with more in speech because if there is a misunderstanding, it's easy to fix. *I should* in the above example is just a short form for *I should study tonight*. We leave out the main part of the verb in speech, but in writing it's best to be complete.

Remember that the verbs *to have* and *to be*, along with all of their various forms (*had, are/was/were*, and so on) can be either helping verbs or main verbs.

Non-Verbs, Disguised as Verbs

Some words look like verbs but are not actually verbs. These words fall into two groups that occur quite often. You need to make sure to avoid confusing these words that *look like* verbs with actual verbs. The two groups are

- phrases with *to* + verb, for example, "**to solve** this problem"
- *-ing* words, for example, "while **making** this argument"

Words like *solve* are not verbs when they immediately follow the word *to*: *to* in front of a verb actually de-verbs the verb. These phrases often appear with actual verbs, but they are not verbs themselves. You will also sometimes see "*in order to* + verb" phrases, such as this: *In order to solve this problem*. Such phrases are not verbs either. Although *solve* can be a verb, it isn't one here.

Words in the second category, *-ing* words, aren't actually verbs on their own; however, they are verbs when they appear after a form of the verb *to be*: *is, are, was, were, will be, have been*, and so on.

Here are some examples:

> I have one goal right now. To graduate next year.

> I'm tired today. Studying until really late last night.

Let's analyze each example.

In the first example above, the first part has a verb: *have*. The second word group, however, does not have a verb: *to graduate* looks like a verb, but as you now know, it isn't. Thus, the second word group isn't a complete sentence. In fact, it's a sentence fragment.

In the second example, again, the first word group has a verb: *I'm* is short for *I am*, so the verb is *am*. The second word group, like the second group in the previous example, also lacks a verb: *Studying* looks like a verb, but remember that *-ing* words must come after a form of *to be* in the same word group in order to be verbs. Again, the missing verb means it is a sentence fragment.

Subjects

Once you've determined that a group of words has a verb, you then need to check to make sure it also has a subject.

The word **subject** can generally mean "topic," as in the subjects you are studying in school, but this definition isn't the one we're using here. When we're talking about sentences and how they work, a subject is the noun or pronoun that either performs the action indicated by a verb or experiences the state of being that is indicated by the verb.

> **subject**
> A subject is the noun or pronoun that either performs the action or experiences the state of being that is indicated by the verb.

As you are probably aware, a noun is a word that refers to a person, place, thing, or concept. Here are some examples of the different categories of nouns:

Category of noun	Example
Person	Rick Mercer
Place	St. John's
Thing	city
Concept	happiness

Pronouns are words that we substitute for nouns to avoid repeating them. In fact, the preceding sentence illustrates the point: *them* substitutes for the earlier *nouns* to avoid repeating the word *nouns*.

Some common pronouns in English include

> I/me/we/us
>
> he/she/him/her
>
> they/them
>
> it

Because pronouns substitute for nouns, they can do almost everything that nouns can do, including functioning as subjects:

> **Rick Mercer** is from St. John's, Newfoundland. **He** is from St. John's, Newfoundland.
>
> **My iPod** broke. **It** broke.

Phrases and Clauses

You know what a word is, but what's a phrase, and what's a clause? The following short table summarizes these terms:

If a word group doesn't have a verb	it's a **phrase**.
If a word group has a verb but doesn't have a subject,	it's still a **phrase**.
If a word group has a verb and a subject,	it's a **clause**.

phrases and clauses Phrases are word groups that lack verbs or have verbs but lack subjects. A clause is a word group that has *both* a verb *and* a subject.

Is a clause a sentence? It depends.

Type the following two groups of words in your word processor exactly as you see here:

> I am cold.
>
> Because I am cold.

If your grammar checking is turned on, your word processor (if you're using Microsoft Word, for example) probably underlined or highlighted the second group of words. This feature indicates that there is a grammatical problem with the second group. The first one, however, is fine.

What's the difference? If you look back at the two groups, you'll see that both begin with a capital, both end with a period, and both have the words *I am cold*.

Both groups have verbs: *am* (remember that *am* is always a verb), which indicates the state of being, in this case, the state of being cold.

Both groups have subjects: the pronoun *I*, which refers to the person experiencing the state of being, in this case, the state of being cold.

The only difference between them is that the second one starts with the word *because*. There is something about this word that is causing your word processor to object to the so-called sentence: without this word, the sentence is fine.

Because is a type of word called a **subordinating conjunction**. Subordinating conjunctions are extremely useful; in fact, you can't express certain thoughts easily without them.

> **subordinating conjunction**
> A subordinating conjunction is a word that introduces subordinate clauses.

However, you also have to be careful with them: unless you know the rules for their use, you can run into problems.

Some of the most common subordinating conjunctions spell out WASABI:

W	when, while, what
A	although
S	since
A	as
B	because
I	if

You should note that these are only some of the more common ones. A more complete list is available in Appendix A on page 267.

A clause that begins with a subordinating word (a subordinating conjunction) is called a **subordinate clause**. A clause that does not begin with a subordinating conjunction is called an **independent clause**.

To remember these terms, it's helpful to think of the meanings of the words *subordinate* and *independent*. Subordinate describes something that is dependent on or reliant on someone or something else: in fact, subordinate clauses are also called **dependent clauses**.

> **subordinate/ dependent clause**
> A subordinate clause has a verb and a subject and also begins with a subordinating conjunction. It cannot be a sentence on its own. Instead, it must be attached to an independent clause. Subordinate clauses are also called dependent clauses.

independent clause
An independent clause contains a verb and subject but does not begin with a subordinating conjunction. It can stand alone as a separate sentence, or it can combine with other clauses.

Independent, in contrast, describes someone or something that functions alone, requiring no additional supports. For example, someone who is financially independent is a person who has enough money so that he or she does not depend on anyone else for financial support.

We are now ready to define the term *sentence*: a sentence is a group of words that contains at least one independent clause. This information explains the third non-sentence at the beginning of the module:

> Because students aren't mature enough to attend college/university right away.

In analyzing this example, first look for verbs. We know that *to attend* isn't a verb. *Aren't* is a verb, though: *are + not*.

Does it have a subject? Who isn't mature enough? The noun *students* is the subject. Because there is a verb and a subject, we know that this group of words is a clause.

However, it starts with the subordinating conjunction *because*, so the verb (*aren't*) and subject (*students*) here are part of a subordinate clause.

Subordinate clauses can't be sentences on their own, so this word group is not a **sentence**.

sentence
A sentence is a group of words that contains at least one independent clause.

It's useful at this point to review our definitions in the table below. Because these concepts are all closely interconnected, we've also included a third column with some reminders about how these definitions connect with other ones:

Term	Definition	Interconnections/Reminders
Phrase	a group of words without a verb, or a group of words with a verb but without a subject	A word group has to have *both* a verb and a subject in order to be a clause.
Clause	a group of words that has a verb and a subject	A clause, unlike a phrase, must have *both* a verb and a subject. A clause can be either independent or subordinate.
Verb	a word that indicates action or state of being	Phrases like *to run* aren't verbs. Words ending with *-ing* are sometimes verbs, but only with a form of *to be* helping them.

Term	Definition	Interconnections/Reminders
Subject	a noun or pronoun that performs the action of the verb or experiences the state of being of the verb	The term *subject* in this sense is very specific: it's not the same thing as a topic, what something is about.
Conjunction	a word that links or joins other groups of words together	There are two important types of conjunctions, and they determine what kind of a clause you have. We discussed subordinating conjunctions throughout this module, and we'll introduce coordinating conjunctions in Module 2.2.
Subordinating conjunction	a type of conjunction that indicates a subordinate clause	Some of the most common ones begin with the letters in the word WASABI.
Subordinate clause	a group of words that has a verb and a subject and also begins with a subordinating word (a subordinating conjunction)	Subordinate clauses are also called dependent clauses; they depend on independent clauses. For this reason, they cannot be on their own. If they are, you have a sentence fragment.
Independent clause	a group of words that has a verb and a subject and does not begin with a subordinating word (a subordinating conjunction)	These clauses are called *independent* because they can be on their own as sentences. They can also attach to other independent and subordinate clauses.
Sentence	a group of words that contains at least one independent clause	Defining a sentence this way is better than using vague terms like *a complete idea* because this way gives you a specific set of tests you can do to check whether a group of words is a sentence.

If we look back to the examples at the beginning of the module, we can now explain why these word groups aren't sentences:

- According to Zacarias.
- In order to become more mature.

The first example has an *-ing* word that isn't combined with a form of *is*, so it's not a verb.

The second example has *in order to become*, which isn't a verb either. Thus, neither group has a verb, so neither group is a sentence.

Correcting Sentence Fragments

You now have all the basic tools to recognize and correct sentence fragments. Let's revisit some examples of sentence fragments from earlier in this module:

> I have one goal right now. To graduate next year.

> I'm tired today. Studying until really late last night.

In both examples, you have a complete sentence followed by a fragment.

The first fragment lacks both a verb and a subject, so we can make it a complete sentence by adding both:

> I have one goal right now. **I want** to graduate next year.

Although you could use the same strategy for the second fragment, because the second fragment is the cause of the effect described in the first part, it would be better to make the fragment a subordinate clause by adding the verb *was*, the subject *I*, and the subordinating conjunction *because*. You can then join the subordinate clause to the independent clause:

> I'm tired today **because I was** studying until really late last night.

These two examples illustrate the basic ways to correct sentence fragments:

1. Turn the fragment into a sentence by adding the missing elements (verb, subject).
2. Turn the fragment into a subordinate clause and join it to a nearby independent clause.
3. Attach it to a nearby independent clause, usually (but not always) with a comma. You may be able to attach the fragment as it is, or you may need to rewrite it slightly.

There are also other ways to join independent and subordinate clauses together, as you'll learn about in greater detail in the next module, particularly in relation to the third option.

Module Checklist

Can I

- [ ] identify verbs?
- [ ] distinguish between verbs and words/phrases that look like verbs?
- [ ] identify subjects?
- [ ] distinguish between phrases and clauses?
- [ ] distinguish between independent and subordinate clauses?
- [ ] distinguish between sentences and sentence fragments?
- [ ] correct sentence fragments?

Looking Ahead

This module is absolutely central to the rest of this book. Many common writing mistakes relate in some way to misunderstandings or gaps involving the concepts here.

As you go through the next few modules, you'll see that they build on these ideas. Most concepts in Part 1 involve this material as well. As you move through the modules in Part 1, you'll see that the following topics all require knowledge acquired here, for example:

- how to refer to other texts using signal phrases (Module 1.3)
- how to write effective thesis statements (Module 1.6)
- how to write effective topic sentences (Module 1.7)

These are just a few examples. In fact, because all writing, whether it's at school, in a job, or in your personal life, involves grammatically correct sentences, you can think of the concepts in this module as connected to writing in general.

Self-Check 2

Refer back to the first self-check at the beginning of this module. Have your ideas changed? What new ideas do you have? Write them out in the chart below.

Based on the objectives at the start, how have my views changed since the beginning of this module?	What new information do I have?

Activities

Before turning to the next module, check your understanding of the concepts and terms of this module by completing the activities below.

1. Go back to the examples that open the module. With a partner, verbally explain why each one is or is not a sentence.

2. Read the 10 word groups below and perform the following three tasks.

   a) Find all verbs and their subjects.

   b) Identify all subordinate and independent clauses.

   c) Identify and correct any sentence fragments. Note that you may want to fix fragments by joining them to the preceding or following sentences, if possible.

      i.   According to Agnesi, students should have to take mandatory math courses in college and university.

      ii.   As a result of their inability to perform basic math tasks correctly.

      iii. This inability causes problems for students.

      iv.   Both in classes and in the workplace.

      v.   Although Agnesi is right to be concerned about students' math abilities, her solution will cause more problems.

      vi.   It is unfair.

      vii. And impractical for colleges to implement.

      viii. While Agnesi's solution addresses an issue that could negatively affect the Canadian economy.

      ix.   She doesn't provide sufficient evidence for colleges to implement her plan.

      x.   Therefore, Agnesi needs to rethink her argument.

3. Read the paragraph below and perform the following three tasks.

   a) Find all verbs and their subjects.

   b) Identify all subordinate and independent clauses.

   c) Identify and correct any sentence fragments.

      Writers must always provide evidence to support their claims. Because claims without support are unreliable. Evidence can have different forms, including citations of reliable sources, statistics, quotations from experts, and so on. Regardless of the type of evidence. Writers require evidence if they want to convince readers of their points. Without evidence, writers only have unsupported claims. Risking evidentiary critiques from their readers. Although writers can sometimes trick uncritical readers with poorly supported points by appealing to their emotions, critical readers will usually object to such arguments on evidentiary grounds.

4. Exchange your work in Activity 3 with a partner and compare and discuss answers. Check your answers against those provided by your teacher.

5. Consider these sentences from a passage in "Students Need a Gap Year." Several word groups are either underlined or italicized. Identify each word group as a phrase, subordinate clause, or independent clause:

a) To solve this problem, *colleges and universities should not admit students directly after high school.*

b) The term "gap year" became well known in North America back in 2000 *when Prince William took time off between high school and university to do volunteer work.*

c) All students can benefit from such time off, time to work, *time to volunteer,* and, most importantly, time to become generally more mature before confronting the demands of college and university, *which require that students be much more independent than they are in high school.*

d) When students start college or university, they often experience quite a jolt: they go from high school graduation through a few months of a summer job straight into a very different educational environment.

e) In high school, they lived at home, and their parents took care of a lot of responsibilities that students suddenly have to take on themselves when they go away to college or university—responsibilities that add stress at the same time as students encounter even more new stress associated with the increased demands of post-secondary education.

f) If students experienced a "gap year" between the end of high school and the start of post-secondary education, they would not encounter all these new stresses at the same time.

g) For these reasons, to make sure that all students are sufficiently mature and ready to meet the challenges of post-secondary education, colleges and universities should all require that students take at least a year off between the end of high school and the start of any additional schooling.

6. Analyze a piece of your own writing in terms of the material in this module. Are there any sentence fragments? Note: your teacher may give you more specific instructions about what to do. If so, follow them carefully.

Linking Sentences

[MODULE **2.2**]

Linking Sentences

Module Objectives

Upon successful completion of this module, you will be able to

1. explain the importance of transitions for ensuring clear writing

2. identify transitions by type

3. correct common errors involving transitions, including punctuation with transitions

4. choose appropriate transitions (with accompanying punctuation) to fit the meanings of sentences

5. edit sentences and paragraphs to improve transitions between sentences

6. combine sentences using transitions, with correct punctuation

7. explain the differences in usage among colons, semicolons, and dashes

8. recognize correct and incorrect uses of colons, semicolons, and dashes

9. write sentences correctly using colons, semicolons, and dashes

Self-Check 1

Read the module objectives above. You've probably encountered some of these terms and concepts before; others, however, will likely be new. In point form, identify what seems familiar and what seems new to you in the chart on the next page.

What do I already know about the topics in this module's objectives?	What seems new to me?

Missing Links

Imagine that a student has written the following paragraph:

Zacarias' argument fails because of serious evidentiary,

practical, and ethical problems. Certainly students may choose

to take a "gap year" if they wish. Colleges and universities

should not force them to do so. Zacarias does have one good

point. She is right that some (though not all) students need

help with the transition from high school to college/university.

Colleges and universities should research ways of working with

both students and their parents to help them develop their

skills, maturity, and independence. Programs could help solve

the problems that Zacarias discusses. Students should be the

ones to decide whether they need them. The point of education

is to give people more choices, not to take them away.

Do you notice anything about this paragraph? Here's a hint: look at the points where the different sentences come together.

Here's an alternative version:

> In conclusion, Zacarias' argument fails because of serious
> evidentiary, practical, and ethical problems. Certainly students
> may choose to take a "gap year" if they wish; however, colleges
> and universities should not force them to do so. Despite the
> problems with her argument, however, Zacarias does have one
> good point: she is right that some (though not all) students need
> help with the transition from high school to college/university.
> To help such students, colleges and universities should research
> ways of working with both students and their parents to help
> them develop their skills, maturity, and independence. Such
> programs could help solve the problems that Zacarias discusses,
> but students should be the ones to decide whether they need
> them. The point of education, after all, is to give people more
> choices, not to take them away.

The first paragraph consists entirely of relatively short, unconnected sentences. These sentences lack transitions. They also lack connecting punctuation, beyond periods ending sentences.

Most English teachers would describe this first paragraph as being "choppy" or as having a "repetitive structure." Too many link-less sentences produce boring, repetitive, choppy writing: reading such writing is like listening to someone play the same note on a piano over and over again.

In addition to identifying these problems, the teacher would likely request that the student vary his or her sentence structure and punctuation, both to eliminate this repetition and to knit the ideas together more effectively.

The second paragraph, in contrast, illustrates what would happen if the writer revised to eliminate the problems described above. Transitions now link ideas, helping signal the connections among them to the reader. More diverse punctuation also helps signal these connections: now there are commas, semicolons, and colons.

These links are often called *transitions*, and they are also sometimes just called *links* or *linking words*. These terms all mean the same thing: they all help the reader move easily from one sentence to another.

If you surveyed English teachers (or even readers in general), they would usually prefer the second paragraph to the first. In a course, the type of writing in the second paragraph would also usually result in a higher grade because it connects the ideas more effectively and flows more smoothly. All in all, the second paragraph demonstrates better writing skills than the first.

Here's the problem: sometimes writers avoid these more complex sentence structures because they aren't confident in their ability to use them correctly. This module is all about helping you learn how to improve your writing by gradually introducing these more complex structures into your writing.

Sentences

As you learned in Module 2.1, a sentence requires at least one independent clause. The simplest type of sentence, then, is a sentence that has only one independent clause, as in these examples:

> I run every morning.
>
> Maria is a student.
>
> Sam has a new crib.

Each of these groups of words has a verb (*run/is/has*); each of these groups of words has a subject (*I/Maria/Sam*). None of these groups of words begins with a subordinating word. Thus, if you type them in your word processor, they won't be underlined or highlighted. These are basic, yet entirely correct, English sentences.

These basic sentences are called **simple sentences**: a simple sentence has one (and only one) independent clause.

You can start expanding simple sentences by adding either subordinate clauses or additional independent clauses.

simple sentence
A simple sentence has one, and only one, independent clause.

Here is an example of a sentence with one independent clause and one subordinate clause:

Because I enjoy exercise, I run every morning.

In this example, we've kept the independent clause. We've also added a second clause, the subordinate clause *because I enjoy exercise*.

Links

If you make note of all the links in the second sample paragraph at the start of this module, you'll get a list like the one in the first column of the table below. Notice that punctuation, where present, has been included.

There are several important points here. First, you should note how each transition, regardless of its structure, relates to the meaning of the sentence it's in. You will find a brief description of each transition's role in the second column of the following table:

In conclusion,	One of the simplest types of transitions, this two-word transition simply signals to the reader that the sentence will begin to conclude/sum up the argument the writer has been making so far. You'll find more information about conclusions in Module 1.8.
	When these transitions open sentences, they usually have a single comma separating them from the rest of the sentence.
; however,	Here is another type of transition. This one indicates a contrast between the first independent clause and the second independent clause (these terms are discussed extensively in Module 2.1).
	This particular type of between-clause transition has a semicolon on the left and a comma on the right. Later on, we'll discuss some ways of varying this pattern.
:	Unlike the other ones here, this transition is a single punctuation mark, called a colon, without words attached to it. Colons are basically pointers: they signal that an important explanation, example, quotation, or other element comes next.
	Note that another example of colon use comes in the explanation about the next transition, directly below.

To help such students,	You'll recall from Module 2.1 that *to* phrases like this one aren't verbs. These phrases often work like the one here does: they link the previous sentence with the next one by linking back with *such students* (a reference to the last sentence) and by linking forward with the idea that the next sentence will be about helping these students.
	The phrase is thus a kind of two-lane bridge between the two sentences.
such	This adjective reminds the reader that the writer is referring to a particular type of student described earlier, as opposed to students in general.
, but	This transition, like *however*, also indicates a contrast, but it does so in a different way. Instead of using a semicolon and a comma, this type of transition just uses a comma, which goes before the transition word coming between the two independent clauses.
, after all,	This two-word transition emphasizes the final sentence. *After all* suggests that in the end, this point is the most important. It's thus an appropriate transition to use in the final sentence.
	Note that unlike the transition *in conclusion*, which opens the first sentence of the sample paragraph, this one actually appears inside the sentence. It's set off from the first and second parts of this sentence with a pair of commas.

You should note that some of these transitions are single words; some are phrases; one, in fact, is simply a punctuation mark. Also, most of these transition words and phrases have punctuation marks attached to them.

We suggest that, instead of thinking of these transitions as separate pieces involving words and punctuation, you think of each one as being like a Lego block: a fixed piece that fits in certain places within sentences.

Opening Transitions

The simplest way to link the end of one sentence to the beginning of the next is to open the second sentence with the transition. Here are some one- and two-word transitions that can open sentences:

In conclusion,	Therefore,	In addition,
First,	However,	Also,
Thus,	Moreover,	Next,

What other ones can you think of? What do they mean?

You can also use longer transitions at the start of a sentence, as in this example from the paragraph at the top of page 172:

> **To help such** students, colleges and universities should research ways of working with both students and their parents to help them develop their skills, maturity, and independence.

How does the opening transition here relate to the previous sentence? Actually, it relates in two ways. The first is this: the idea of helping students, expressed by the phrase *to help*, links with the word *help* in the previous sentence. Starting a sentence with *to* + ___ is one way to create such transition, especially when what follows the *to* relates specifically to the last sentence.

What's the second? If you look closely, you'll also see the word *such*. This word also provides an additional link back to the previous sentence. The writer could have left this additional transition out but decided to include it to link back to the phrase *some students* in the last sentence. By including it, the writer has created a stronger link between the two sentences.

Like all transitions that open new sentences, all of these transitions also have a comma that signals the end of the transition and the start of the rest of the sentence.

Types of Transitions

Consider the following pairs of sentences:

Mark is 5'11".	Yesterday was sunny.	Johnson's proposal would solve our problems.
Jake is 5'9".	Today it's pouring rain.	He needs to provide more evidence to support his points.

These pairs of sentences have a particular relationship with each other. The first two pairs involve contrast. The last pair, meanwhile, involves a type of contrast called a concession: the first sentence points out a good quality of the proposal, but the second points out an aspect of the proposal that needs improvement. Thus, the good side and the needs-improvement side contrast with each other.

Skilled writers usually include words that make these kinds of content relationships clearer to their readers. There are various families of these words, but we're going to call them all **transitions**; however, they also have more technical names.

transitions
Transitions link words, phrases, and clauses.

Common transitions		
Coordinating conjunctions	**Subordinating conjunctions**	**Conjunctive adverbs/ transitions**
for	when, while	however
and	although	moreover
nor	since	thus
but	after, as	therefore
or	because	nevertheless
yet	if	in addition
so		additionally

A more complete list is available in Appendix B on page 268.

You've already encountered the words in the first column: you'll remember from Module 2.1 that these words are subordinating conjunctions. If you've already read Module 1.3, you've also encountered the word *as* in one of the signal phrase patterns.

> As you learned in Module 2.1, you can remember the common subordinating conjunctions using WASABI. Also, you can remember the coordinating conjunctions using FANBOYS.

These words are arranged in three groups because the words in each group behave similarly with regard to punctuation—the subject of the rest of this module. We should note that they behave similarly but not identically.

Like all members of families, in fact, there is some variation, as we'll address in Module 2.3. Treat the examples and advice here as guidelines; they are not always absolute rules.

As you become more advanced as a writer, you will encounter situations where flexibility is possible. For now, though, we suggest that you follow these guidelines.

Phrases, Clauses, Transitions, and Punctuation

Here are several different ways to combine the earlier sentence pairs using the words from the table directly above:

With a coordinating conjunction:	With a subordinating conjunction:	With a conjunctive adverb/transition:
Mark is 5'11", but Jake is 5'9".	Although Mark is 5'11", Jake is 5'9".	Mark is 5'11"; however, Jake is 5'9".
Yesterday was sunny, but today it's pouring rain.	Although yesterday was sunny, today it's pouring rain.	Yesterday was sunny; however, today it's pouring rain.
Johnson's proposal would solve our problems, but he needs to provide more evidence to support his points.	Although Johnson's proposal would solve our problems, he needs to provide more evidence to support his points.	Johnson's proposal would solve our problem; however, he needs to provide more evidence to support his points.

As you can see, there is a pattern here. In each of the three families of connecting words, the connecting words have similar patterns in terms of their position in the sentence and the punctuation marks that go with them.

For the first family of words, coordinating conjunctions, we've only used *but* in the above examples. Actually, however, coordinating conjunctions behave similarly: when they go between two independent clauses, they follow a comma. Here is the pattern:

_____, connector _____.
      Independent Clause #1   Independent Clause #2

Johnson's proposal would solve our problems, but he needs to provide more evidence to support his points.

Words in the second family, subordinating conjunctions, behave differently. These words often open sentences, like this:

Connector _____, _____.
           Subordinate Clause #1   Independent Clause #1

Although Johnson's proposal would solve our problems, he needs to provide more evidence to support his points.

Finally, the third family is quite different from the other two. These words combine with both a semicolon and a comma when they join two independent clauses within a single sentence, like this:

_____ ; connector, _____.
  Independent Clause #1   Independent Clause #2

Johnson's proposal would solve our problem; however, he needs to provide more evidence to support his points.

You can also use a period to separate the two independent clauses into separate sentences:

_____ . Connector, _____.
  Independent Clause #1   Independent Clause #2

Johnson's proposal would solve our problem. However, he needs to provide more evidence to support his points.

Semicolons, Colons, and Dashes

The Semicolon (;)

The second-last example sentence in the previous section uses a semicolon to join two clauses. People sometimes fear the semicolon, but actually, its basic pattern is fairly simple: a semicolon generally joins two balanced independent clauses.

In this case, *balanced* means that the two clauses should be equally important. In the second-last example sentence from the previous section, for example, the first independent clause states a point about Johnson's proposal. The second independent clause, meanwhile, adds an additional point about Johnson's proposal.

The relationship here is contrast: the writer contrasts the benefits of Johnson's proposal with areas in which it needs improvement. The two points are different, and neither explains the other.

The Colon (:)

Colons, in contrast, are quite different. Colons do not balance sentences: instead, they introduce a second word, phrase, or independent clause that explains, illustrates, elaborates on, or completes the first. You will see a colon used in this way whenever writers introduce a list or a quotation, for example. In fact, you will probably remember that one of our signal phrase patterns from Module 1.3 uses a colon for this reason.

Writing that deals with arguments and evidence will often have more colons than semicolons because the situations that require colons are more common: argumentative writing often provides explanations, elaborations, examples, and so on. These are all elements that you can emphasize by leading into them with colons.

The Dash (—)

A dash can also be used to join clauses. First, a dash is not the same as a hyphen. Its appearance and function are both different.

Different word processors will form dashes in different ways. However, your word processor will usually merge two short hyphens into a longer, continuous horizontal stroke—a dash. If not, don't worry. The two hyphens will still form an acceptable dash.

In terms of its function, think of a dash as an extra-emphatic colon. Like a colon, a dash points at what comes next, drawing the emphasis forward. However, a dash provides more emphasis than a colon.

Thus, dashes are useful when you want to provide extra emphasis. However, it's best to just use them occasionally. Too much emphasis is just as bad as not enough—emphasizing everything is like emphasizing nothing.

Avoiding Common Mistakes with Semicolons, Colons, and Dashes

Don't Use a Semicolon When a Colon Is a Better Fit

As the previous section states, one common mistake with semicolons occurs when writers use them where colons would better fit the meaning of the sentence:

> Agnesi's argument ignores the different math needs of students in more technical programs; engineering students, for example, require much more advanced math skills than students in certain other fields.

The second independent clause here provides new information that explains the more general statement in the first independent clause. In such situations, colons are more appropriate, as the emphasis should fall more on the second clause.

The writer might also consider using a dash here; however, a dash would only be a good choice if he or she hadn't already used one nearby.

Don't Use Colons with Words That Function Like Colons

Colons are like arrows; however, certain words and phrases have the same pointing function because of their meaning. Because these words and phrases mean the same as a colon, don't combine them with colons—doing so is redundant. Examples of these words/phrases include:

include/includes/included/including	like
such as	for example

Sometimes writers also use colons after words like *have* or *having*. Again, these words don't require a colon because the words that follow are so closely connected that you shouldn't separate them with a colon.

For instance, all three colons in the following example sentence are incorrect:

> For example: problems with Agnesi's argument include: her poor use of evidence and her overgeneralization of students as having: poor math skills.

Instead, you can replace the first colon with a comma (after the opening transition) and eliminate the others:

> For example, problems with Agnesi's argument include her poor use of evidence and her overgeneralization of students as having poor math skills.

Sometimes you can use the words like those in the list above in a sentence that has a colon: it's important, though, that the colon does not directly follow the word. Here is an example:

> Problems like this one are common in argumentation: too often writers will jump to conclusions based on insufficient evidence.

Finally, because dashes behave like extra-emphatic colons, you should also avoid dashes after the words/phrases in the above list.

Don't Overuse Dashes

Sometimes writers overuse punctuation marks that they have recently learned, as in this example, which overuses dashes to the point of distraction:

> Agnesi's argument ignores the different math needs of students in more technical programs—engineering students, for example, require much more advanced math skills than students in certain other fields. In addition, such students probably enter with much better math skills than the average student—their program requires such skills—as a result, students without good math skills tend not to be accepted.

This example uses three dashes in six lines, two of which appear in the same sentence. Such overuse makes it seem like the writer is banging his or her fist on the table. You should revise such passages to eliminate the excess dashes.

Sentence Fragments, Revisited

Let's return briefly to a topic from Module 2.1: correcting sentence fragments. Now that you've learned about colons and dashes, you have another way of correcting certain types of fragments. Because colons and dashes can join phrases to independent clauses, you can use them to pull some fragments into a nearby independent clause, as in this example from page 162 in Module 2.1:

> I have one goal right now. To graduate next year.

You could, as we suggested then, make the fragment its own independent clause by adding a subject and a verb, but you can also join the phrase to the preceding independent clause with a colon:

> I have one goal right now: to graduate next year.

You could also use a dash, depending on how much emphasis you want:

> I have one goal right now—to graduate next year.

This last piece of advice, in fact, reveals why it's useful to learn about different types of punctuation: with additional knowledge, you gain additional options in your writing.

Module Checklist

Can I

☐ use a range of transitions, with their accompanying punctuation?

☐ correct common errors involving transitions?

☐ use a range of punctuation marks to create variety by linking sentences, including commas, semicolons, colons, and dashes?

☐ avoid common errors with semicolons, colons, and dashes, by

  ☐ using a colon instead of a semicolon where a colon would better fit the meaning?

  ☐ omitting colons after "arrow" words like *such as*, *include/included/ including*, and *for example*?

  ☐ using dashes sparingly?

  ☐ correcting sentence fragments?

Looking Ahead

Because these connecting words allow writers to join several clauses together in one sentence instead of separate sentences, these words are especially well suited for writing thesis statements and topic sentences: both thesis statements and topic sentences often require writers to link together statements in this way.

For instance, in a critical response essay, one type of thesis might look a lot like the example involving Johnson's proposal that we looked at in the table on page 178. This sentence acknowledges a good feature of Johnson's proposal, but it also makes a critical statement about how it can be improved.

By linking the two thoughts together with these connecting words, you create a smoothly flowing, grammatically correct sentence that sets up the rest of your essay—and you get marks for doing it. This smooth flow between sentences is called cohesion, which we also discuss in relation to body paragraphs in Module 1.7.

Self-Check 2

Refer back to the first self-check at the beginning of this module. Have your ideas changed? What new ideas do you have? Write them out in the chart below.

Based on the objectives at the start, how have my views changed since the beginning of this module?	What new information do I have?

Activities

Before turning to the next module, check your understanding of the concepts and terms of this module by completing the activities below.

1. Find examples of correctly used transitions and punctuation marks described in this chapter in readings from your other courses. Examine the transitions. Look at how they illustrate the principles of effective transition use that we've discussed in this module.

2. Insert the appropriate punctuation marks in the blanks provided:

   a) When Zacarias accuses "students" of being "too immature to start college or university right after high school" _____ she issues a blanket insult to all students.

   b) Moreover _____ Zacarias provides no proof that this alleged immaturity affects enough students to justify requiring everyone to take a year off.

   c) A "gap year" would potentially cost students a lot of money _____ however _____ Zacarias provides no concrete evidence that it would have much effect on student maturity.

   d) Some students would probably gain significant maturity in a year _____ but other students would probably remain largely unchanged.

   e) Agnesi's argument has a major problem _____ she does not convincingly establish the existence of a general, serious problem with students' math skills.

3. Insert the appropriate transition words/phrases in the blanks provided, along with any necessary punctuation:

   a) Zacarias accuses "students" of being "too immature to start college or university right after high school"; _____ she issues a blanket insult to all students.

   b) Zacarias _____ provides no proof that this alleged immaturity affects enough students to justify requiring everyone to take a year off.

   c) _____ a "gap year" would potentially cost students a lot of money, Zacarias provides no concrete evidence that it would have much effect on student maturity.

d) Some students would probably gain significant maturity in a year; _____ other students would probably remain largely unchanged.

e) Agnesi's argument has a major problem _____ she does not convincingly establish the existence of a general, serious problem with students' math skills.

4. Insert the appropriate transitions and punctuation marks in the blanks provided. In some cases, different answers may be possible. If you think you've come up with an answer that doesn't fit into the blanks, ask your teacher for guidance. Note: some words may need capital letters.

> Transitions between words, phrases, and ideas help writers clarify the connections between ideas _____ _____ they also help readers understand these connections. _____ writers sometimes think that the connections between ideas are obvious _____ they are not _____ _____ writers need to work to ensure that their transitions are effective. _____ transitions are missing _____ readers can have difficulty figuring out the relationship among the ideas. _____ _____ missing transitions can suggest that the writer didn't understand how the ideas related to each other _____ the result can be a loss in credibility for the writer.

5. Combine the following groups of independent clauses using transitions, with correct punctuation. Depending on the situation, you may choose to leave one or more clauses as a separate sentence and combine others, or you might choose to combine all the clauses into one sentence. Note that different options/combinations are possible.

a) I want to go out tonight. I can't. I have to study for my midterms.

b) Zacarias' argument has serious flaws. Her proposal requires revision. We cannot take it seriously.

c) Zacarias' proposal would discriminate against students from less privileged economic backgrounds. These students cannot afford to spend a year travelling the world. Tuition rises each year. Delaying school for a year means paying increased tuition. Students will end up paying more for their diplomas.

d) Agnesi proposes that all students have poor math skills. She overgeneralizes about all students by lumping them all together in one group.

e) Agnesi uses the term *students*. This word implies "all students" or "students in general." Her language here is offensive to students. It accuses all students of having weak skills. Only some actually do.

6. Exchange your answers from Activity 5 with a partner. Compare and discuss any differences in your revised sentences.

7. The following four sentences are from a paragraph that contains several mistakes involving punctuation marks with transitions. Identify the mistakes and correct them. Note that there may be more than one mistake per sentence.

a) Despite Agnesi's good intentions; her proposal's flaws make it impossible to consider without major revisions.

b) Aside from problems with evidence, her proposal has other serious flaws; it is both impractical and unethical.

c) Because—Zacarias does not acknowledge that students have different maturity levels when they begin college; she dooms her argument from the start.

d) However she may have a point when she suggests that students may require additional time to mature.

8. Rewrite the following paragraph to eliminate the choppy sentences: combine them using the transitions and punctuation marks described in this module.

> Agnesi is correct to be concerned about students' math ability. Her proposal that all students should take math is flawed in several ways. She provides no evidence that students in general have gaps in their math skills. Some students likely have excellent math skills. Students in different programs likely have very different math needs. Students in engineering or computer science will require different math skills than a student in law. Agnesi proposes a single course for everyone. This solution lumps all students together and ignores the differing needs of students. A better solution would be to conduct research on students' math readiness in terms of their different program requirements and propose a solution that takes these differing needs into account. Programs will have specific evidence about specific gaps. They will be better equipped to help students succeed.

9. Choose a piece of your own writing (it doesn't have to be from the course using this book). Analyze your use of transitions in light of the advice given in this module. How might you improve your use of transitions? Use the module checklist in your analysis.

More on Commas

[MODULE **2.3**]

More on Commas

Module Objectives

Upon successful completion of this module, you will be able to

1. recognize the problems with common myths regarding comma use
2. recognize sentence structures related to comma use
3. apply selected principles regarding comma use
4. edit sentences containing a variety of comma errors

Self-Check **1**

Read the module objectives above. You've probably encountered some of these terms and concepts before; others, however, will likely be new. In point form, identify what seems familiar and what seems new to you in the chart below.

What do I already know about the topics in this module's objectives?	What seems new to me?

Myths about Comma Use

Have you ever heard that you should always put a comma before the word *and*? Or that you should put a comma wherever you would pause or take a breath?

Are there any other pieces of advice you've heard regarding commas? What are they?

Here's the bad news: these so-called rules don't work. They might result in correct commas sometimes, but they are just as likely to result in incorrect ones. Here's the good news: this module provides advice regarding comma use that does work.

Why shouldn't you always put a comma before the word *and*? To begin, *always* is an awfully strong word and should make you ask, "Really? *Always*?" Second, the real problem here is that the word *and* appears in several different kinds of situations. Some of these situations require commas, and some do not. In fact, if you look over this paragraph, you'll see examples of *and* both without and with a comma. Which ones are right? Actually, they all are, but in order to explain why, we have to explain a little more grammar.

The problem with the second so-called rule—and the reason why it's a myth— is that *most* punctuation marks indicate a pause, and these are pauses of varying lengths. A situation where you would pause in a sentence *might* require a comma; on the other hand, it might require a semicolon, as this sentence did. There are other situations, too: sometimes you want a colon. Still other situations require a more emphatic pause—such as with a dash. Finally, each sentence ends with a pause of some kind: a period, a question mark, or an explanation point! Got it?

We've already described these other punctuation marks, so in general, you know when to use them. We've also already introduced a few selected comma rules as part of our sentence building blocks in the last module. Next, we're going to expand our rules about comma use to cover several extremely common situations.

Commas with *And* (and Family)

As you know from the last module, *and* belongs to a family of words called coordinating conjunctions. When *and* joins two independent clauses, you should include a comma, as in this example:

> Zacarias provides insufficient evidence for her argument, **and** she also neglects students' rights.

This pattern applies to any sentence with *and* joining two independent clauses:

> ____IC1___, and____IC2___.

This rule becomes even more powerful when you realize that it also applies to all words in the *and* family—in other words, to all coordinating conjunctions. You'll find these words listed below:

F	For
A	And
N	Nor
B	But
O	Or
Y	Yet
S	So

> The first letters of the seven coordinating conjunctions spell out FANBOYS, or if you change the order slightly, SONYFAB.

Here are examples using two of the more common coordinating conjunctions, *but* and *so*:

> Zacarias has students' interests in mind, **but** her approach would actually hurt students.

> Zacarias' proposal lacks evidence, **so** we should not accept it.

In fact, we can now make this general pattern:

> ____IC1___, coordinating conjunction ___IC2___.

A Few Exceptions

There are other patterns where you also want to use a comma with *and*. First, however, let's discuss several situations where *and* does *not* require a comma.

Sometimes a sentence can have more than one noun or pronoun as part of the subject:

> Andrea and I are meeting today after class.

This sentence has a three-word subject: the noun *Andrea* and the pronoun *I* joined by *and*. You can actually have as many nouns/pronouns in a subject as you want (though we'd recommend against making your subjects too long). Here's an example:

> Andrea, John, and Craig have formed a study group.

You may have noticed that *and* doesn't have a comma in the double subject, but commas re-appear in the triple subject in the second example. In fact, you should generally leave out commas from double subjects.

Don't use commas before *and* in double subjects.

These comma-less *and* situations appear with other double structures as well:

> I run and swim every morning.
>
> I am an avid hiker and kayaker.
>
> I texted Andrea and Craig 20 minutes ago.

However, if we add a third verb to the first example here, or if we add a third noun/pronoun to the other two, the doubles become triples, and the commas re-appear:

> I run, swim, and lift weights every morning.
>
> I am an avid hiker, rock climber, and kayaker.
>
> I texted Andrea, John, and Craig 20 minutes ago.

Use a comma before *and* (and other coordinating conjunctions as well) when *and* joins two independent clauses.

Don't use a comma before *and* when *and* joins double nouns/pronouns or verbs.

Do use commas when *and* joins triple nouns/pronouns or verbs in a series.

In real-world writing, of course, these rules combine with other rules:

> Because Zacarias' argument has serious evidentiary, ethical, and practical problems, we should not implement her proposal, but students and colleges should explore additional research on ways to improve students' readiness for college. Moreover, this research should be both evidence based and should propose practical solutions for all students.

Please go through and number the commas in the paragraph above. The chart below explains each comma in terms of the rules we have discussed so far:

Paragraph	Comma rule shown
Because Zacarias' argument has serious evidentiary,₁ ethical,₂ and practical problems,₃ we should not implement her proposal,₄ but students and colleges should explore additional research on ways to improve students' readiness for college. Moreover,₅ this research should be both evidence based and should propose practical solutions for all students.	Commas 1 and 2: commas in a triple series. Comma 3: comma separates opening subordinate clause from independent clause. Comma 4: comma before a coordinating conjunction (*but*) between two independent clauses. Comma 5: comma after a transitional word (*Moreover*) or after an expression that begins an independent clause. You should recall this kind of comma from Module 2.2 (page 179).

Note that in the first sentence, *students and colleges* has no comma before *and* because *and* here is part of a double subject.

Note as well in the last sentence that there is no comma before *and should propose* because this *and* is part of a double verb: (1) *should be . . .* (2) *and should propose . . .*

Patterns and Punctuation

The examples above follow predictable patterns. These patterns help you avoid relying on myths about breaths and pauses. After all, if you try to add a comma any time you'd take a breath, you won't be following a predictable pattern at all. You won't always feel the need to "pause" in the same place in your writing, and your classmates won't always feel the need to "take a breath" in the same place as you.

Transitional Word/Phrase + Comma

When you use an introductory element like *moreover* (in the Comma 5 example above) or *however*, you do need to add a comma after it. You add it in this case not only because you need to pause but also because these introductory words are separate elements (or building blocks) of the sentence structure.

Here is an example:

> I had hoped to visit Nova Scotia and New Brunswick this summer. However, I used the money to replace my old car.

Subordinate Clause + Comma

Although—like other subordinating conjunctions such as *because* and *if*—attaches to the words that follow it to make an entire clause subordinate (dependent). Subordinating conjunctions such as *although* do not stand alone as transition words, so the comma comes later on in the sentence at the end of the full subordinate (dependent) clause.

Here is an example:

> Although I had hoped to visit Nova Scotia and New Brunswick this summer, I used the money to replace my old car.

Adding a comma after the word *although* would not be correct because the entire opening subordinate clause is a single unit that you should not split up.

Sometimes subordinate clauses can follow independent clauses. Subordinate clauses that start with *although* can't usually do so, but other subordinate clauses can, especially ones beginning with *because* or *if*. When a subordinate clause follows an independent clause, there is no comma between the two clauses.

> I couldn't visit Nova Scotia and New Brunswick this summer because I used that money to replace my old car.

This situation is different from words like *however* and *moreover*: these words simply link an independent clause to a preceding clause, but subordinating conjunctions are tightly built into the subordinate clause and should not be separated from the rest of the clause.

Instead of worrying whether or not you need to add a comma when you pause, carefully follow the advice in this module to find the pattern to figure out where the comma needs to go.

Module Checklist

Have I

- [ ] identified common myths about comma placement?
- [ ] used a comma before *and* when I have three or more items in a list of nouns, pronouns, or verbs?
- [ ] used a comma before coordinating conjunctions when they separate two independent clauses?
- [ ] used a comma to separate the end of an initial subordinate clause from an independent clause that follows it?

Looking Ahead

Because commas have so many different uses, they are among the most difficult of punctuation marks to master. What you have learned in this module will be helpful in the later module on general editing and revising.

Of course, commas appear in writing every day, and with the basic rules provided in this book, you'll likely be more comfortable figuring out where to put commas in things you write for other courses and in your personal and professional life.

A more comprehensive writing handbook will set out additional rules that build on the ones here.

Self-Check 2

Refer back to the first self-check at the beginning of this module. Have your ideas changed? What new ideas do you have? Write them out in the chart below.

Based on the objectives at the start, how have my views changed since the beginning of this module?	What new information do I have?

Activities

Before turning to the next module, check your understanding of the concepts and terms of this module by completing the activities below.

1. Which of the following commas are correct? Which ones are incorrect? Are any missing? (Some of these example sentences come from earlier in this module, so after you are done, you can look back and check your work.)

   a) I run, swim and lift weights every morning.

   b) We should not implement her proposal but students and colleges should explore additional research on ways to improve students' readiness for college.

   c) In fact, if you'll look over this paragraph, you'll see examples of *and* both without and with a comma.

   d) Although, I had hoped to visit Nova Scotia and New Brunswick this summer I used the money to replace my old car.

   e) When *and* links together two independent clauses you should include a comma before the *and*.

2. Insert any necessary commas in the blanks provided. If no comma is required, leave the blank empty.

   a) I am planning on taking a trip to Jasper____ Banff____ and Glacier National Parks this summer.

   b) While I was waiting for the bus this morning____ I saw an accident between a red car____ and a blue pick-up truck.

   c) I think it is important for people to vote in municipal elections____ however____ very few candidates seem to represent my point of view.

   d) Although____ my train was four hours late____ my family was still waiting for me to take me home for Christmas break.

   e) Smith____ and Barnsley make some good observations about the increasing cost of tuition____ but they forget about all of the other rising costs that students face such as food____ rent____ and books.

3. Analyze the first paragraph in the section "Looking Ahead" above. Find each comma and explain its use in terms of the rules and patterns covered in this module.

4. Read through the paragraph below and add any commas that are missing.

> Post-secondary students in Canada pay far too much for their education. Because of the rising cost of tuition fewer students in the future are going to be able to save enough money to go to college or university. Part-time work is not as plentiful as it used to be because more people are competing for the same number of jobs. Furthermore minimum wage is nowhere near enough money to live on while attempting to save for school. Some families will have enough savings to help pay for tuition rent and food but many more students will be left trying to finance their diplomas and degrees through student loans. Unfortunately when the students graduate from college or university they will be saddled with extraordinary financial troubles. At that point students will need to find good-paying jobs to pay back the government the banks and the credit card companies that have loaned the students the money. However many students are finding it difficult to make ends meet with entry-level positions right after college or university. If this trend keeps going students are not going to be able to pay back their loans and the Canadian taxpayers as a whole are going to be stuck with the bill. We ought to look at reducing the cost of enrolling in post-secondary education if we want to serve the long-term economic interests of all Canadians.

5. Look at the essay you've been preparing in the Activities from Modules 1.6 to 1.8. Find each comma that you've used and check to see if you've placed it correctly. Make any necessary changes to your work.

6. Your teacher will distribute an article to you. As in Activity 3, you should identify each comma that you see and explain which rule is being followed by the writer. Are there any commas that this module doesn't explain? What are they? If you want, try to find the answer by checking a writing handbook or asking your teacher.

Common Punctuation Errors

[MODULE 2.4]

Common Punctuation Errors

Module Objectives

Upon successful completion of this module, you will be able to correct a range of punctuation errors, including

1. comma splices and fused sentences
2. incorrect and ineffective semicolons
3. incorrect colons
4. incorrect or missing apostrophes

Self-Check 1

Read the module objectives above. You've probably encountered some of these terms and concepts before; others, however, will likely be new. In point form, identify what seems familiar and what seems new to you in the chart below.

What do I already know about the topics in this module's objectives?	What seems new to me?

Teachers, Students, Errors, and Grades

How many punctuation errors can you spot in the following passage?

> According to: Mae Agnesi, students' should have to take a mandatory math course in college and university, because many students don't have the math skills they need for their future jobs. She states, that student's can't do simple arithmetic, and cites the example of a student who couldn't figure out a basic percentage score on a test. Although, Agnesi is right to be concerned about students' math skills; her argument has several serious problems, including: poor use of supporting evidence, inattention to practical issues, and no consideration of potential ethical problems. Agnesi does not address these problems, no one should take her proposal seriously.

There are quite a few errors in this paragraph. In fact, it is only 104 words long, yet it has 10 different punctuation errors—in other words, there is a mistake every 10 words or so.

Now imagine one of your teachers reading one of your papers. Your paper effectively summarizes sources; it has a well-developed introduction, body, and conclusion, and a critical thesis. However, it also contains a significant number of errors in punctuation, like the ones in the passage above.

Here is what is probably going to happen. Your teacher, instead of being uniformly impressed, has to start balancing these mistakes against the good points in determining your mark. Your mark thus starts dropping relative to what it could have been.

Errors

Before we start talking about these errors in detail and linking them with earlier concepts, it is worth thinking briefly about the term *error* and what it means.

Error basically means "mistake," but if you look more deeply at the word, it used to be connected to a word that means "wander," as in "to wander off." In fact, mistakes do involve wandering away from the rules, true, but they also cause your reader's attention to wander away from what you're saying. Since the purpose of punctuation (and grammar, in general) is to support what you're saying, such wandering is a fairly serious failure of communication. As we state above, this problem results in lost marks.

Students sometimes find these lost marks unfair, often thinking frustrated thoughts like this: why can't the teacher see through these mistakes to what I'm saying? Since your teachers are the ones giving the marks, it helps here to see things from their perspective.

Now imagine another paper that is equally good in terms of all the same features *and* contains no punctuation errors. In this case, the teacher does not have to see past anything: the punctuation supports the content, instead of undercutting it. This second paper is always going to get a higher mark because it has more things done properly than the first one.

Punctuation, as we have explained in previous modules, exists to support writing, the same way road signs exist to help people find their way. Incorrect punctuation distracts the reader at best, and at worst, may actually result in confusion about what you are saying.

This module will help you avoid such distraction and confusion by extending the previous modules about commas, colons, semicolons, and dashes. Those modules are all about how to use these punctuation marks correctly. This module, however, explains common mistakes, why we think students make them, and, most importantly, how to avoid them.

Commas

Punctuation marks tend to function as signposts and connectors: they tell us where a sentence is going, and, in combination with transitions, they tell us how the different parts of the sentence relate to each other.

Commas are particularly troublesome in this regard because they are correct in a wide range of different situations. Earlier modules in Part 2 are about these situations, so we won't repeat all of that material here.

Instead, this section addresses a common and serious error called a comma splice and a related error called a fused sentence. Both of these errors involve the incorrect connection of clauses; sometimes these problems are also called "run-on sentences."

We will also return briefly to the "pause myth" from Module 2.3 because this myth also relates to a common additional error with commas.

Comma Splices

You have learned various correct ways of joining together clauses: with words like *and*, with words like *moreover*, and with words like *although*, just to name a few. What is not correct, though, is to join two independent clauses together using a comma *alone*, as in the last sentence from the passage that opens this module:

> Agnesi does not address these problems, no one should take her proposal seriously.

Any English teacher would circle the comma here and write "**comma splice**" ("CS"). Some teachers may use the term *comma fault*, but it's the same idea.

This is one of those moments in which you might be wondering why teachers can't pay attention to your content instead of obsessing about commas. There are two answers to this question.

> comma splice
> A comma splice occurs when you link together two grammatically independent clauses with just a comma.

The first is a practical one: it's the teacher's job to make sure that your writing does not contain errors that will distract your reader from understanding what you are saying. This answer alone, however, is of course unsatisfactory.

The second and more important answer is this: loosely linking two grammatically independent clauses with just a comma, the vaguest and most general of marks, clouds the connection between the ideas. It's as though the writer doesn't care how they relate—or worse, doesn't know.

Thus, the teacher in our example above *is* paying attention to your content by paying attention to your use of commas! If you've linked together two ideas incorrectly, the ideas themselves are no longer clear: the relationship between these two ideas has become confused, and the structure of your argument suffers. The content you've worked so hard to present in your essay unravels because of the faulty commas.

Comma splices occur commonly before words like *however*, *moreover*, and other conjunctive adverbs (see the chart on page 177). However, conjunctive adverbs are usually followed by a correct comma. In the following example, the first comma has incorrectly joined two independent clauses while the second one correctly follows the conjunctive adverb:

> Personal experience is not necessarily good evidence, however, it can be effective in some situations.

The first comma in the example above has created a comma splice.

As you learned in Module 2.2, the best way to punctuate the above example is to place a semicolon before the conjunctive adverb *however*, which joins the independent clauses. You need to pay attention to the pattern:

INDEPENDENT CLAUSE + [semicolon] + conjunctive adverb + [comma] + **INDEPENDENT CLAUSE**

By remembering this punctuation pattern, you can not only recognize comma splices when you see them but also correct them.

There are also more complex cases involving comma splices that you should note. To spot comma splices in these more complex situations, you should treat a word group containing an independent clause and a subordinate clause (or clauses) as though it is a single independent clause: this word group cannot correctly link to the remainder of the sentence with a comma. Here is an example of this situation:

> Agnesi's argument is flawed because she omits valid evidence, moreover, her overgeneralizations about students invite objections from critical readers.

The clause immediately before the first comma is a subordinate clause ("because she omits valid evidence"), but that subordinate clause is in turn attached to an independent clause. The comma before *moreover* is still spliced, and it should be fixed with a semicolon as in the previous example with *however*:

> Agnesi's argument is flawed because she omits valid evidence; moreover, her overgeneralizations about students invite objections from critical readers.

Fixing Comma Splices

Fortunately, your grammar checker will usually catch comma splices. Also fortunately, you can avoid spliced commas—or fix them if you splice one by mistake and notice afterward—by simply following the advice given in earlier modules, which present numerous correct alternatives.

1. You can make the two clauses separate sentences:

> Agnesi does not address these problems. No one should take her proposal seriously.

Personal experience is not necessarily good evidence. However, it can be effective in some situations.

We suggest, however, that you not overuse this option because your writing will be choppy as a result.

2. You can replace the comma with a semicolon or colon, depending on what fits the meaning of the sentence. Remember that when you use a semicolon, you should try to strengthen the link between the two independent clauses with a transition word:

Agnesi does not address these problems; thus, no one should take her proposal seriously.

Personal experience is not necessarily good evidence; however, it can be effective in some situations.

3. You can keep the comma and add a coordinating conjunction (see page 178 to review this pattern):

Agnesi does not address these problems, so no one should take her proposal seriously.

Personal experience is not necessarily good evidence, but it can be effective in some situations.

4. You can make one of the clauses subordinate by adding a subordinating conjunction, thus making the comma correct (see page 178 to review this pattern):

Unless Agnesi addresses these problems, no one should take her proposal seriously.

Although personal experience is not necessarily good evidence, it can be effective in some situations.

We should mention one special case in which you can correctly place a comma on its own between two independent clauses:

Agnesi presents weak evidence, she neglects practical concerns, and she ignores ethical objections.

Because the first comma here is part of a *series* of independent clauses, it's correct to use it alone between independent clauses. To review the use of commas in a series, you can check page 193 in Module 2.3. In this case, the comma is fine.

Fused Sentences

fused sentence
A fused sentence occurs when you link together two grammatically independent clauses with no punctuation at all.

There is a relatively rare type of error called a **fused sentence** that we should explain before we move on:

> Agnesi does not address these problems no one should take her proposal seriously.

A fused sentence is a kind of comma splice in reverse: just as you cannot join two independent clauses with a solitary comma (something), you also cannot join them with blank space (nothing).

The example above runs the two clauses (*Agnesi does not address these problems* and *no one should take her proposal seriously*) together. In other words, it fuses them.

If you added just a comma at the connection point between the two clauses (between *problems* and *no one*, in this case), you would then have a comma splice. As you'll remember from the last section of this module, this comma is incorrect by itself, but it provides a starting point.

In order to fix fused sentences, you should follow one of the four patterns that we used to avoid or fix comma splices on pages 206–207, and you will have a correct sentence.

Finally, as you learned in Module 2.3, one common myth about comma use is that you should insert a comma wherever you pause. The following incorrect comma from the opening passage illustrates the problems that can result from this myth:

> Although, Agnesi is right to be concerned about students' math skills . . .

Although you may well pause after *although*, you should not put a comma in this position. Remove it.

Semicolons

As Module 2.2 points out, a semicolon should hinge together two independent clauses that you want to emphasize equally. As shown earlier in this module, semicolons are a common way to *fix* comma splices. Although they can solve punctuation problems, sometimes semicolons themselves are the problem.

Semicolons only work in certain positions in certain sentence structures, so writers need to be highly aware of structure when they use them. However, writers sometimes put them where they simply don't belong, as in the following example:

> Although Agnesi is right to be concerned about students' math skills; her argument has several serious problems . . .

Note that the opening clause is subordinate, not independent, so the semicolon between *skills* and *her* should actually be a comma.

Such problems often result from inattention rather than misunderstanding: the writer, deep into the sentence, forgets that the opening clause isn't independent, doesn't look back to check, and incorrectly inserts a semicolon.

There is another problematic situation that we should note: sometimes writers will use a semicolon when a colon would be a much better choice for the sentence. In such situations, although the semicolon is technically correct, it is not the best choice.

In fact, the first sentence in the preceding paragraph illustrates this point. What if the writer used a semicolon instead of a colon, as in this altered version of the first sentence from that paragraph?

> There is another situation that we should note; sometimes writers will use a semicolon when a colon would be a more effective choice for the sentence.

The semicolon is correct here in the sense that it's between two groups, each containing an independent clause. However, because the second part of the sentence *explains* the first, a colon better supports this situation by pointing to the explanation.

In general, it is best not to use a semicolon when the second part of the sentence explains or elaborates on the first. In such situations, a colon (or even a dash) is better. See Module 2.2 for more information about these punctuation marks.

Colons

The passage that begins this module has two errors involving colons. The first error occurs in the opening signal phrase:

> According to: Mae Agnesi, . . .

First, as you may recall from Module 1.3, this signal phrase does not have a colon: the comma following the signal phrase is correct, but the colon is not. Colons, as you will recall from Module 2.2, go after an opening independent clause, and *according to* isn't a clause at all.

You may be interested to learn that despite these two different ways of explaining why the colon is incorrect, this error is a relatively common one. We suspect that students, having correctly learned that colons point to and thus emphasize information that comes next, misapply this principle to this situation. Yes, the phrase *according to* does point to the author's name, but the other rules about colon use make this colon incorrect.

The second incorrect colon is here:

> ... her argument has several serious problems, including: poor use of supporting evidence, inattention to practical issues, and no consideration of potential ethical problems.

The structure of this sentence is relatively complicated, but to explain why this colon is incorrect, you only need to know this principle: words and phrases like *include* (and variants like *including*), *for example*, and *such as* by definition point to what comes next. A colon also points to what comes next. It's neither necessary nor correct to point twice.

Errors with Apostrophes

Apostrophes do two main things: they indicate possession and they indicate contractions. For example, this apostrophe indicates that the argument belongs to Agnesi:

> Agnesi's argument has several problems.

The same idea applies to things:

> This argument's flaws are clear to any reasonable reader.

What about a name ending in *s*, like *Zacarias*?

> Zacarias' argument has several problems.

When words end in *s*, it's easiest to just put an apostrophe after the *s* when forming the possessive. The same principle applies to plural possessives:

> These arguments' flaws are clear to any reasonable reader.

You will usually see possessive forms of nouns before other nouns: Agnesi's argument, the argument's flaws, Zacarias' argument, arguments' flaws.

Writers often leave out these apostrophes. Remember to check to make sure that you've included them where necessary.

Sometimes writers mistakenly put apostrophes in other places, perhaps because they see an *s* and think an apostrophe is necessary:

> Agnesi argue's that all college students should have to take math.

This apostrophe is incorrect. This situation doesn't involve possession at all; it doesn't even involve a noun. In fact, *argues* is a verb. Remove it:

> Agnesi **argues** that all college students should have to take math.

If you're typing, your grammar checker will usually catch these problems, but if you're writing by hand, you will need to watch out for them yourself.

Apostrophes also appear in contractions, shortened combinations of words, usually involving *not* and *are*:

> can't, won't, shouldn't, isn't, weren't, I'm, they're . . . and more

Writers don't often make mistakes with these words, and again, your word processor will usually detect them. However, writers very often get confused about the word *it's*. *It's* is short for *it is*:

> It's [it is] not fair to require that all students take a year off before they attend college or university.

It's only ever means *it is*, and if *it is* doesn't make sense in the situation, then you know that *it's* is wrong:

> The car broke it's axle.

The car broke it is axle makes no sense. In fact, what you want in the above example is the possessive form of *it*—*its* without an apostrophe:

> The car broke its axle.

Finally, sometimes writers will try to create a new word *its'*. There is no such word in the English language. It's never correct—not ever.

Module Checklist

Have I ensured that my writing is free of these common errors?

- ☐ comma splices or fused sentences
- ☐ incorrect (or missing) commas
- ☐ incorrect semicolons
- ☐ semicolons that should be colons
- ☐ incorrect colons
- ☐ incorrect (or missing) apostrophes

Looking Ahead

As we've noted, this module looks back over the first few modules in Part 2, particularly with regard to clauses (2.1) and how they link together (2.2). It also looks forward to all the writing you will do during the rest of your life.

The punctuation marks—and their accompanying common errors—that we survey here will keep occurring as long as people keep writing. The skills needed to prevent punctuation errors from occurring (and to recognize and correct them when they do) will continue to be important and relevant.

Meanwhile, closer to the present, this material will play a big role in Module 2.8, which is about editing, revising, and proofreading.

Self-Check 2

Refer back to the first self-check at the beginning of this module. Have your ideas changed? What new ideas do you have? Write them out in the chart below.

Based on the objectives at the start, how have my views changed since the beginning of this module?	What new information do I have?

Activities

Before turning to the next module, check your understanding of the concepts and terms of this module by completing the activities below.

1. a) Identify the punctuation errors in the following sentences. Note that some sentences may contain more than one error, and some sentences may be entirely correct:

    i. Effective evidence is entirely missing here: for example: Agnesi cites no studies, statistics, or any other valid, verifiable information.

    ii. The idea that student's would become significantly more mature after a gap year requires convincing evidence, unfortunately, Zacarias provides none.

    iii. Valid evidence for her claims would include such things as: reliable statistics, published sources, and experts' statements.

    iv. This proposal may have some merit; however, its' flaws require correction before anyone can take it seriously.

    v. According to Zacarias; a gap year would help students' because it would allow them to gain additional maturity before they attend college or university, in addition, because such maturity would in turn improve their ability to succeed in their studies: it would improve their chances to be successful in life.

   b) Compare your answers with a partner's. Are they the same? Are any answers different? Discuss.

   c) Correct the errors in each of the above sentences.

2. a) Identify the punctuation errors in this paragraph:

    As Agnesi states; math is important for all future jobs, including: servers, nurses, and many others. According to Agnesi, many students lack basic math skills, thus, she argues that math should be required for everyone in college and university. This arguments' flaws should be clear to any reasonable person; first, it's not logical to use Agnesis own cherry-picked personal experiences as evidence for general statements about students math skills. Second, she neglect's to consider any practical details about these courses and how they would work. Finally, an argument based on a negative overgeneralization about students is unethical. For all of these reasons: Agnesis' proposal should not go forward; however, individual programs should review their requirements to ensure that their students are graduating with the math skills that they need to succeed in their future jobs.

b) Compare your answers with a partner's. Are they the same? Are any answers different? Discuss.

c) Correct the errors in the above paragraph.

3. Review your own writing, either for this course, another course, or both. The essay you were writing during the course of Part 1—especially in Modules 1.6 to 1.8—would be a good option for this activity. Have you made any of the errors described in this module? Which ones? Find examples and correct them.

Agreement

[MODULE **2.5**]

Agreement

Module Objectives

Upon successful completion of this module, you should be able to

1. describe the concepts of pronoun reference, pronoun agreement, and subject–verb agreement
2. explain the importance of clear pronoun use in writing
3. edit sentences to correct common errors with pronoun reference, pronoun agreement, and subject–verb agreement

---

Self-Check 1

Read the module objectives above. You've probably encountered some of these terms and concepts before; others, however, will likely be new. In point form, identify what seems familiar and what seems new to you in the chart below.

What do I already know about the topics in this module's objectives?	What seems new to me?

Don't Disagree

Most of us have probably become confused in conversations like this one:

Person 1: Pass that to me, would you?

Person 2: What?

Person 1: THAT. Pass it to me?

Person 2: What? I don't know what you mean.

Person 1: That folder, the red one. Please pass it to me.

Person 2: Oh, okay, here you go.

That? That what? In speech, you can fix such confusion by doing exactly what our imaginary conversation participants do above: the second person asks for more information, the first person eventually provides it, and all becomes clear. In writing, however, you can't ask for clarification in this way.

The confusion here comes from problems with unclear pronoun reference.

Here is a different (though related) situation. You would never write a sentence like this one:

Mae Agnesi argue that students need math for their future jobs.

Clearly *argue* here should be *argues*. However, sometimes with more complicated situations, the choice isn't as clear:

The many problems with Agnesi's argument includes her failure to provide any compelling evidence regarding students' math problems.

If you type this sentence into a word processor, the grammar checker (assuming it's turned on) will identify a problem with the verb *includes*. Can you explain what it is? If you're thinking that it should be *include*, you're right, but can you explain why?

The key issues here involve two related concepts called *reference* and *agreement*.

Reference and Agreement

Pronouns, as you may know already, substitute for nouns. We use pronouns constantly, mostly to avoid repeating nouns over and over again. We also use pronouns to refer to things when we don't know what the thing in question is actually called, as in this question: *What's that?*

You can use a noun in one part of a sentence, and refer back to this same noun with a pronoun that appears later in the sentence. Pronouns thus jump across multiple words to link up with earlier nouns: in this way, you can think of pronouns as empty containers that need nouns to fill them with meaning.

For example, consider this sentence:

> When **Agnesi** argues that everyone needs a math course, she overgeneralizes about students.

In this example, the pronoun *she* clearly refers back to the noun *Agnesi*. After all, words like *she*, *it*, and *this* (to name just a few pronouns) do not mean much on their own: without nouns to fill these empty containers, you would be permanently confused.

pronoun reference
The term *pronoun reference* describes how a pronoun refers to a particular noun.

Pronouns, in other words, generally need to point or refer to nouns, and this concept is called **pronoun reference**. When they fail to point clearly, confusion arises, as in the example with the red folder above.

In addition to referring clearly to a specific noun, pronouns also need to match up with this noun in certain ways. Consider this sentence:

> Robin drove down the desert highway. They were glad that the car had air conditioning because the temperature outside was over a hundred degrees.

The first sentence mentions only Robin, but the next sentence introduces the pronoun *they*, which cannot be used to refer to a single person. Without more information explaining who *they* are, readers will be rather confused by this unusual shift from one person to a pronoun that refers to more than one person. We also expect *he* or *she*, not *they*, because *Robin* is one person.

pronoun agreement
Pronoun agreement describes how singular pronouns refer to singular nouns and plural pronouns refer to plural nouns.

This expected matching between a pronoun and the noun that completes the picture is called **pronoun agreement**. Basically, singular pronouns need to refer to singular nouns and plural pronouns need to refer to plural nouns.

You can think of this principle as the one-to-one/many-to-many rule.

More on Pronouns

Here are some common pronouns:

Referring to people	Referring to things	Referring to both
I/me	this/that	they/them
he/she/him/her	these/those	
you	that, which	
who/whom/whose	it	

As a writer, you need to know when and how to use these pronouns and also how to avoid common problems with them.

The most important thing to keep in mind is this: pronouns are useful because they can refer back to nouns, but this feature also requires writers to be careful, as pronouns can sometimes seem to refer to more than one noun, resulting in confusion for the reader.

As we've said before, confused readers mean that the writer has been unsuccessful. In addition, pronoun problems can also suggest confusion in the mind of the writer about the ideas, and you do not want to give this impression either!

Consider this example:

> I'll hold the nail, and when I nod my head, hit it with the hammer.

Here is a more complicated example:

> Attach component A to component B with the red cable. Then, attach it to component C with the attached connector pins.

Is it completely clear what *it* is in both cases? In the first case, because *it* is closer in the sentence to the noun *head*, it looks like the speaker is asking the other person to hit his head with the hammer. Clearly, though, the context tells you that *it* refers to the nail. In fact, this first example is an old joke, and the humour comes when the listener or reader realizes the funny lack of clarity here.

In the second example, however, can you tell what the *it* is? What are you attaching to component C? You can't figure out from the context what the writer means. You might be able to figure out what the writer means by looking carefully at the components and the cable and thinking about how they should connect, but at that point, the instructions are useless—the whole point of instructions is that they are supposed to stop you from having to puzzle things out in this way.

Here's the key idea: a pronoun needs to clearly refer to a single noun. Otherwise, you can confuse your readers. The noun a pronoun refers to is sometimes called its antecedent (meaning "what comes before"), its referent, or its target.

Avoiding Broad Pronoun References

The examples above illustrate a problem called broad or unclear pronoun reference, or broad pronoun references (BPR) for short.

Broad also means *wide*, and wide is a good way to think of the problem here. The pronouns in the examples above can refer to different nouns, so it's like someone pointing at a wide area with several items on it. Which one is the person pointing at? It can be hard to tell. The same problem exists with broad pronoun references.

Writers can avoid broad pronoun references in several ways.

To keep things clear, you should place pronouns as close as possible to the nouns to which they refer. Avoid having other nouns in between the pronoun and its target noun.

> I'll hold the nail; you hit it with the hammer when I nod my head.

Now the pronoun *it* only has one possible target earlier in the sentence: *nail*.

You can also reword the sentence by using a noun instead of a pronoun:

> I'll hold the nail, and when I nod my head, hit the nail with the hammer.

You might also decide to shorten the sentence, like this:

> When I nod my head, hit the nail with the hammer.

In the case of the example about the components, the easiest option is to replace the pronoun with a noun. When pronouns cause unclear writing, sometimes avoiding them completely is the best option:

> Attach component A to component B with the red cable. Then, attach component A to component C with the attached connector pins.

There are a few other more specific types of broad pronoun references that we'll discuss next.

Problems with *This, That, These, Those,* and *Which*

Some words can cause particular problems: *this, that, these, those, which.* These words can be unclear in the same way as *it;* however, there are different ways to fix them.

Consider the following example.

> Zacarias' argument suffers from a lack of evidence. This is a serious problem because her argument is less credible as a result.

This *what?* Readers don't know what the target noun for *this* is, because there are three nouns in the preceding sentence: *argument, lack,* and *evidence.* The closest is *evidence.* So what is the "serious problem"? It's not the argument. It's not evidence. The problem is the *lack* of evidence. To make this point clear, you can rewrite the sentence like this:

> Zacarias' argument suffers from a lack of evidence. This lack of evidence is a serious problem because her argument is less credible as a result.

The usual solution to problems with *this* (and the related words) is always to follow *this/that/these/those* with a noun or phrase that clarifies the target. If you're thinking that this approach leads to repetition, you're right, but repetition is better than confusion every time.

Of course, if you would rather not add a noun/phrase after *this,* you can also eliminate the pronoun completely with a full rewrite:

> Because Zacarias fails to present evidence, her argument is less credible as a result.

There is an exception to this principle. When *this* leads directly into the target (usually with a colon or a dash), you do not need a noun following it, as the target directly follows, as in this example:

> The most important objection to Agnesi's argument is this: because she does not prove that post-secondary students have problems with math, her proposal is a solution in search of a problem.

There is no confusion here because the colon directly links the pronoun and its target: the *this* refers to the paraphrase of Agnesi's argument that comes immediately after it.

Similar problems can occur with the pronoun *which*:

> I don't know how to swim, which is a problem.

Which refers back to which noun? If you look carefully at the first part of the sentence, there actually aren't any nouns in it for the pronoun to target. Pronouns need to refer back to specific nouns, so using *which* to refer generally (and vaguely) to the entire idea of the previous clause is not a good idea.

To avoid the broad reference, you can rephrase the sentence in several ways:

> I have a problem: I don't know how to swim.

> I don't know how to swim, so I have a problem.

When there are several options for how to rephrase your sentence, it's usually a good idea to avoid too much repetition. Instead, use different options in the interest of sentence variety (see Module 2.2 for a discussion of how to vary your sentence structure and punctuation). For example, with regard to the examples of different revisions above, if the sentence immediately before the rephrased sentence also uses a colon, you might decide to use the second option to avoid repeating this colon right away.

Pronoun Agreement

You already know quite a lot about pronoun agreement, even if you don't know the term. You don't use *he* to refer to a woman, you don't use *they* to refer to one person, and you don't say *me hungry* (at least not since you were very young).

What about this example? Try typing the following sentence into your word processor with your grammar checker turned on:

> Everyone must turn off their cell phones during the test.

In fact, we wrote this book using Microsoft Word, and in the document, the word *their* in this sentence is underlined in green. Your word processor may indicate a grammatical mistake differently, but it should indicate it. If you ask the computer for help, Word suggests replacing *their* with *his or her*. Why?

Words like *everyone* are called indefinite pronouns. They do not substitute for earlier nouns in the same way as other pronouns do; however, they do arguably substitute in the sense that a noun like *everyone* substitutes for *all* people in a certain category—for example, everyone reading this book, everyone attending college, and so on.

Here is a list of common indefinite pronouns:		
anyone	everyone	someone
anybody	everybody	somebody

A more complete list is available in Appendix C on page 269.

Indefinite pronouns are singular. Refer back to them using *he or she*, or *his or her*, as fits the particular sentence. For example, instead of using *their* to refer back to *everyone*, you would use *his or her*:

> Everyone must turn off his or her cell phone during the test.

Alternatively, you might simply avoid *everyone* completely, like this:

> All students must turn off their cell phones during the test.

In this second example, the writer has replaced the singular indefinite pronoun *everyone* with the plural noun *students*, so *their* is now correct.

Often, avoiding indefinite pronouns (as in the example above) leads to clearer, less awkward writing.

However, there will be times when you have to use indefinite pronouns, and in such cases, always link back to these words with *he or she*, *his or her*, or *him or her*, as necessary.

Subject–Verb Agreement

Subject–verb agreement is similar to pronoun agreement. Let's return to the example sentence from the beginning of the module:

> The many problems with Agnesi's argument includes her failure to provide any compelling evidence regarding students' math problems.

The verb here is *includes*, which is singular. You know from Module 2.1 (page 157) that the subject is the noun or pronoun that performs the action or indicates the state of being indicated by the verb. So you can ask this question: what exactly includes her failure to provide any compelling evidence? Her *failure* is a problem, one of several, according to this sentence.

In fact, the word *problems*, which is plural, is actually the subject of the verb *includes*. When your grammar checker highlights or underlines the verb *includes*, here, it's telling you that the singular form of the verb doesn't agree with its plural subject.

Prepositional Phrases

You may find the phrase in between *problems* and *includes* to be confusing. Why, people sometimes ask, isn't *Agnesi's argument* the subject? Doesn't it also include the problem that the second part of the sentence describes?

The following diagram illustrates the relationship between *problems* and the phrase *with Agnesi's argument*:

> The many **problems** . . . **include** . . .
>
> > with
> >
> > Agnesi's
> >
> > argument

This three-word phrase, as this diagram suggests, isn't the subject; instead, it's actually a sub-component *of* the subject that simply gives more information. In fact, you could take it out completely and you would still have a grammatically complete sentence:

> The many problems include her failure to provide any compelling evidence regarding students' math problems.

However, try deleting the phrase *the many problems*, and you get this:

> with Agnesi's argument includes her failure to provide any compelling   •
> evidence regarding students' math problems.

Clearly this version isn't a grammatically complete sentence. In fact, it doesn't make sense.

Phrases with words like *with*, *about*, *of*, and others, called prepositional phrases, often correctly appear in the same position—that is, between verbs and their subjects.

Remember, though, that you don't want the verb to agree with anything inside these in-between phrases. Look back past the prepositional phrase to the actual subject. Usually thinking about the meaning will help you.

Mistakes with subject–verb agreement are very easy to make even when you know the rules. People have a tendency to make the verb agree with the closest noun, whether that noun is the subject or not. In fact, one of the authors of this book used to be prone to this error, especially in first drafts.

The good news is that your word processor's grammar checker is fairly good at catching these mistakes. Even so, these word-processing tools are not always reliable, so you should be especially careful to look for and correct these errors—see Module 2.8 for more information.

There are many other kinds of subject–verb agreement errors—in fact, a more detailed handbook will usually have many pages of rules about subject–verb agreement. For now, however, you know the basics. Your teacher may decide to add to the information here, especially if he or she discovers that you are making errors not specifically covered here, so be sure to keep your notes carefully up to date.

Module Checklist

Have I

- ☐ checked that each pronoun
    - ☐ clearly refers to the intended target?
    - ☐ agrees with the intended target?

- ☐ checked that each verb agrees with its subject and not with some other word or phrase?

- ☐ edited my sentences to remove errors with:
    - ☐ pronoun agreement
    - ☐ pronoun reference
    - ☐ subject–verb agreement

Looking Ahead

We are now well into the second part of this book. You've now gained, we hope, a deeper knowledge of sentence structure, transitions, punctuation, and some basic concepts about verbs and pronouns.

The topics in the next module, modification and parallelism, draw on concepts similar to the ones presented here. A module on avoiding wordiness will follow. Finally, Part 2 ends with a module on revision, which ties everything together via a discussion of editing, revising, and proofreading. You will want to keep in mind how to fix the kinds of errors that we've discussed throughout Part 2.

You will keep writing long after you finish that final module, however, and as you continue to write (in other courses and at work), you may at times need to look up points of grammar and punctuation in reference books. This book provides some foundational knowledge and terms that you will need to use such reference books effectively.

Self-Check 2

Refer back to the first self-check at the beginning of this module. Have your ideas changed? What new ideas do you have? Write them out in the chart below.

Based on the objectives at the start, how have my views changed since the beginning of this module?	What new information do I have?

Activities

Before turning to the next module, check your understanding of the concepts and terms of this module by completing the activities below.

1. a) First, underline the nouns and pronouns in the following paragraph:

   According to Louise Zacarias, every student should be required to take a year off before they begin college or university. Zacarias says this because she claims that students are too immature to start post-secondary studies right away. According to her, it causes problems when they go right into college or university because their behaviour can be immature, which causes problems for them and they get into trouble. Zacarias feels that her proposal will help solve this. However, her proposal will cause its own problems. The most serious of these problems are her proposal's likely effect on student finances. Most students in Canada is not able to afford to take a "gap year," and if they are forced to take one, they will experience financial hardship as a result.

   b) Which of the pronouns in the paragraph above are correct? Which ones are incorrect? Why?

   c) Exchange your work with a partner. Check each other's work.

   d) Rewrite the paragraph in (a) so that all pronouns are correct. Remember that you may need to do more than just plug in different pronouns to fix the problems.

   e) Exchange your rewritten paragraph with a partner. Check each other's work and then discuss your revisions.

2. a) Underline the verbs and their subjects in the above paragraph.

   b) Next, repeat Steps 1(b) through 1(e) for the above paragraph, but this time with the verbs.

3. a) The following paragraph contains various problems with both pronouns and subject–verb agreement. Identify and correct all problems. Tip: start by identifying all pronouns, all their targets, all verbs, and all their subjects. Then, go through them all one by one.

   A large number of grammar and punctuation problems distract the person reading a piece of writing. If you write in a way that distracts your reader, your writing is not effective, and they may dismiss your writing because it has too many mistakes. It is a big problem if this happens because all writers need to make sure that they keep their readers' attention focused on his or her content, not focused on mistakes, which will happen if there is mistakes every second or third word.

b) Exchange your rewritten paragraph with a partner. Check each other's work.

4. Choose a piece of writing that you have done recently. (You may decide to pick the essay that you were working on throughout Modules 1.6–1.8.) Are there any issues with pronoun reference, pronoun agreement, or subject–verb agreement? What are they? Fix the issues using the principles from this module. If you have any questions, ask your teacher.

Modification and Parallelism

[MODULE **2.6**]

Modification and Parallelism

Module Objectives

Upon successful completion of this module, you will be able to

1. explain the importance of correct modification patterns and parallel structures to clear writing
2. correct modification errors in sentences
3. correct faulty parallel structures in sentences

Self-Check 1

Read the module objectives above. You've probably encountered some of these terms and concepts before; others, however, will likely be new. In point form, identify what seems familiar and what seems new to you in the chart below.

What do I already know about the topics in this module's objectives?	What seems new to me?

Matching: Modifiers and Targets

Consider the following sentence:

> Barking, howling, and scratching at the door, my neighbour was woken up by his dog.

The opening word group is not a clause. Remember from Module 2.1 that *-ing* words are not verbs unless a form of *is* comes before them. A group of words without a verb is a phrase, so we have an opening phrase that describes various noises made by a dog, followed by an independent clause that explains that the writer's neighbour's dog woke him up.

The phrase *barking, howling, and scratching* has a particular role in the sentence: it tells us what kinds of noises the dog is making. This opening phrase is called a **modifier**. Modification simply means description: thus, a modifier is simply a word or word group that describes another word or word group.

> **modifier**
> Modifiers are words or phrases that describe other words or phrases.

There is, in a fact, a problem with the modification in the above sentence: the opening phrase is modifying the wrong noun. In order to explain why, we need to explain how modification works.

Before we do so, though, we would like to point out another feature of the opening phrase—something so obvious, in fact, that you perhaps didn't even notice it: parallelism.

You may know the word *parallel* from geometry, where it describes lines tilted at the same angle so that they never touch. In writing, **parallelism** refers to a sequence of words or phrases with the same form. In this case, notice the parallel endings:

> **Parallelism**
> Parallelism refers to a sequence of words or phrases with the same form.

> Barking, howling, and scratching . . .

We usually don't notice parallelism when it's done correctly: the repetition of the forms simply carries us along. When parallelism isn't done correctly, however, we notice: it's like two odd socks, or a sudden wrong note on a piano. Something doesn't fit, and this lack of fit distracts the reader. We'll say more about parallelism after we discuss modification in greater detail.

Modification Errors

Lazy Modifiers and Misplaced Targets

In a sense, modification resembles pronoun reference and agreement and subject–verb agreement: all of these grammatical principles involve a word or a group of words linking up with another group of words and agreeing with it in some way.

As we have seen with subject–verb agreement, verbs match their subjects in terms of being singular or plural: a singular subject takes a singular verb, and so on. With modifiers, however, this linking up is more complicated: modifiers link up with other words in sentences by describing them.

This description, in turn, must make sense. Because every modifier must modify something, you need to look to make sure that a modifier doesn't modify the wrong thing—in other words, you need to make sure that the modifier and its target link up correctly and match in terms of the intended meaning.

In the sentence that opens the previous section, the writer definitely *means* that the barking, howling, and scratching is being done by the dog. However, there is a problem: the modifier is at the beginning of the sentence, the target of the modifier is at the end, and there is another noun in between: *neighbour*.

Modifiers are lazy: they attach to whatever potential target comes closest to them. Thus, the sentence is actually saying that the writer's neighbour was barking, howling, and scratching at the door, and that while he was engaged in this dog-like behaviour, his actual dog woke him up somehow.

You may be thinking that the writer clearly didn't mean to suggest that the neighbour was barking, howling, and scratching at the door: the clear intention is that the dog was doing so and that the dog's noise woke up the neighbour. The problem is this: what the writer meant isn't what the writer said.

Readers expect modifiers to link up clearly with their targets, and when they don't, the reader must stop and figure out what the writer means. At best, the reader has to pause and regroup; at worst, the reader may be confused or even misled.

If you can't imagine such a situation, here's one. Suppose a police officer is taking notes after a car accident. In this accident, Joe turned left illegally and struck Alex. However, according to the report,

> After turning left illegally, Alex was struck by Joe.

This sentence now states the opposite of what actually happened. Moreover, unlike the sentence with the neighbour and dog, you can't figure out the likely meaning from the context.

Modification problems aren't limited to phrases involving *-ing* words. They can also happen with *to* (or *in order to*) phrases, like this one:

> In order to print documents, the paper tray must be completely closed.

In this sentence, the writer means that the *printer* requires a properly shut paper tray in order to print anything. However, the same modification problem that you've seen in the examples above exists here. A paper tray doesn't print anything: it simply holds paper. The printer does the printing. In other words, the modifier here is linking up with a target that doesn't make sense.

People sometimes think that insistence on correct modification is overly picky. In the above example, everyone knows what the person means, right? Maybe. However, we need to keep three important things in mind.

First, modification errors often reveal both carelessness with grammar and, even worse, sloppy, imprecise thinking. Second, they can distract your readers. Third, and most importantly, in certain situations (such as instructions or descriptions of situations like the traffic accident above), they can cause genuine confusion.

Modification errors can also lead to odd statements:

> To visit my grandmother, the car first needs to be fixed.

Unless your grandmother is looking forward to a visit from your car instead of you, you don't want to write the sentence this way. Again, yes, the intended meaning is arguably clear, but readers shouldn't have to work around your writing to get to what you're trying to say.

These kinds of errors usually happen because writers shift gears mentally between the modifier and the target—they think of something else connected with the situation at hand, and this other word/phrase intrudes. This shift causes the writer to reverse the target with another word, putting the sentence out of joint.

Fixing Modification Errors

To fix such problems with modification, you need to rewrite the incorrect sentences so that the target appears in the correct position, directly after the modifier:

> In order to print, **the printer** must have its paper tray completely closed.

> To visit my grandmother, **we** first need to fix the car.

There are almost always other solutions as well, but they usually involve much more extensive rewriting:

> You should close the paper tray completely before you print.

This new version changes the sentence structure so that there is no longer a modifier-plus-target, just two completely separate clauses, the first independent, the second subordinate.

You should be especially careful with *by* structures because they tend to occur fairly often when writers combine summary with critical response, as in this example:

> By proposing that all students take math, Agnesi's overgeneralization insults the many students with strong math skills.

The writer of this example sentence would like *Agnesi* to be the target of the opening modifier here. It is Agnesi who proposes that all students take math. However, because of how the above sentence is constructed, *Agnesi's overgeneralization* is the target. This modification error is a problem because an *overgeneralization* cannot propose anything. Only a person can.

You should also note that *by* phrases at the beginnings of sentences need to be set off by a comma and followed by a noun (or pronoun) that makes sense as the target. Sometimes people start with *by* and then mistakenly scramble the sentence structure, like this:

> By proposing that all students take math insults the many students with strong math skills.

This sentence now has a completely incorrect structure.

To fix it, you can do one of two things. One solution would be to restore this proper structure:

by + modifier_____ [comma] [correct target] _____
  [phrase beginning with an *-ing* word]   [noun]

When applied to this situation, the above structure looks like this:

> By proposing that all students take math, Agnesi insultingly overgeneralizes about students with strong math skills.

You can also just rewrite the sentence. In this case, we could do this:

> Proposing that all students take math insultingly overgeneralizes about students with strong math skills.

Without *by* and within a slightly revised structure, the word *proposing* is now the subject of a clear and concise sentence rather than a confusing modification problem at the start of a broken sentence.

You can also rewrite the sentence more extensively, like this:

> Agnesi's overgeneralized proposal that all students should take math insults students with strong math skills.

Numerous other revised versions are of course also possible.

When checking modifiers for errors, you should first locate the modifier, if there is one, and then locate the target. Next, ask yourself whether the description makes sense. If the sentence structure has humans scratching at doors or cars visiting grandmothers, you need to rewrite the sentence—except, of course, in the unlikely event that you meant what you wrote.

Parallelism

Word groups in sequence need to be parallel as well. To illustrate how jarring faulty parallelism can be, this example shows the original sentence from this module with the modification error fixed but with the opening parallelism broken:

> Barking, howling, and because he was scratching at the door, my neighbour's dog woke him up.

One of these things is not like the others. The first two elements (*Barking, howling*) are still parallel; however, the third element in the modifier now wanders off into a longer, different structure, throwing the entire opening phrase off balance and out of parallel.

Although parallelism is important everywhere, it tends to come up particularly often in thesis statements, especially the sort where people list multiple points in sequence:

> Zacarias fails to provide evidence, consider practical problems, and she is unethical.

These points are all good ones: Zacarias' argument certainly does have all of these weaknesses. The sentence itself, however, is a jumble. We have the phrases *fails to provide, consider*, and *is unethical*. The first two phrases match, as the word *provide* in the first phrase parallels the word *consider*. However, the third phrase is completely out of alignment with the first two.

How would you revise this sentence? One way to fix parallelism problems is to ask what all the elements have in common. In this example, all three points involve what Zacarias doesn't do, so you might rewrite the sentence so that the verb phrase *fails to* leads into three parallel points:

> Zacarias fails to provide effective evidence, consider practical problems, or address ethical issues.

Now all three elements have the same structure: *provide effective evidence* (verb + adjective + noun), *consider practical problems* (verb + adjective + noun), and *address ethical issues* (verb + adjective + noun).

You could also revise the sentence in a completely different way:

> Zacarias' argument has evidentiary, practical, and ethical problems.

This second version is also parallel. In this case, we have revised the sentence so that we've presented Zacarias' flaws as three adjectives modifying the noun *problems*. Other options are also possible.

Problems with parallelism can be tricky to solve: sometimes trial and error is needed. However, if pressed for time, you might also consider dividing the points into separate sentences. Parallelism problems are less common when the points aren't next to each other in a sequence, and you can then expand each sentence to explain the individual points in more detail, as in this example:

> Zacarias' argument has evidentiary problems: she does not back up her points with anything beyond her personal experience. Also, by failing to include any details about how such mandatory math courses would work, she ignores practical issues. Finally, her argument overgeneralizes about students and is thus unethical.

There is no rule that says that three (or more) points have to be sequenced in the same sentence, but if they are, they should be parallel.

In fact, you shouldn't necessarily think of the two options as either/or choices. The longer and more detailed option can work well in an introduction, in which you need to set out and explain points systematically before developing them even further in your body paragraphs. The shorter option, meanwhile, can be useful for linking back to earlier points during the restatement phase of a conclusion.

For more information on introductions, bodies, and conclusions, see Modules 1.6, 1.7, and 1.8.

Module Checklist

Have I

☐ verified that all modifiers match up with the correct targets?

☐ checked that opening phrases with *by* are properly punctuated and structured?

☐ checked that words and phrases in sequence are parallel?

Looking Ahead

In a sense, this module looks in both directions, back and ahead, because it relates both to writing you will do in the future and to some relatively early modules in Part 1 of this book.

When it comes to the essays that you have been assigned to work on for this and other classes, different options regarding parallel structure affect how you write introductions, how you set up body paragraphs, and how you link back to earlier points in conclusions. The clarity of your ideas will be helped immensely by having parallel language and properly modified sentences.

With regard to the future, correct modification and parallelism are basic features of good writing, so as long you write, you will need to pay attention to these concepts or risk distracting and confusing your readers.

Self-Check 2

Refer back to the first self-check at the beginning of this module. Have your ideas changed? What new ideas do you have? Write them out in the chart below.

Based on the objectives at the start, how have my views changed since the beginning of this module?	What new information do I have?

Activities

Before turning to the next module, check your understanding of the concepts and terms of this module by completing the activities below.

1. Underline the modifiers and circle the targets in the sentences below. Note that some modifiers may not have targets. If they don't, the lack of a target is a problem that you should note in Activity 2.

   a) By proposing that all students take math, Agnesi risks forcing students to take unwanted courses that may delay their graduation.

   b) To address Zacarias' argument, several supporting points deserve criticism.

   c) By arguing without evidence is a proposal that we should not support.

   d) After presenting several paragraphs of evidence, his essay concludes with a restatement of the initial thesis.

   e) To support this point, Agnesi provides only her own personal experiences.

2. a) Which sentences above contain modification errors? Which ones are correct? Why?

   b) With a partner, explain each of your answers to (a).

3. a) Rewrite the incorrect sentences from Activity 1 so that they are correct.

   b) Exchange your rewritten sentences from (a) with a partner. Compare your decisions.

4. Identify any instances of faulty parallelism in the following sentences by underlining the words or phrases that are not parallel. If the sentence correctly uses parallel language, place a check mark beside it.

   a) Zacarias' argument has poor use of evidence, it is overgeneralized, and impracticalities don't get mentioned.

   b) Risking lower numbers of successful graduates and higher numbers of discouraged students, Agnesi insists on mandatory math even though she lacks evidence to support her proposal.

   c) Alternatives to Zacarias' proposal include making a gap year optional and students' parents and high schools should do a better job preparing them for college.

d) This proposal, despite its good intentions, is unsupported, impractical, and unfair.

e) Agnesi's insistence on mandatory math ignores the needs of students, fails to consider what different programs require in terms of math skills, and doesn't help the students' future employers either.

5. With a partner, discuss each of your answers to Activity 4 with reference to the content of this module.

6. a) Rewrite the incorrect sentences from Activity 4 so that they are correct.

   b) Exchange your rewritten sentences from (a) with a partner. Compare your decisions.

7. a) The following paragraph contains several examples of correct and incorrect modification. It also contains correct and faulty parallelism. Identify the problems and correct them by rewriting the sentences in which the problems occur.

   > Agnesi is right to consider the needs of students, but by insisting on mandatory math courses for everyone, students would experience a lot of inconvenience as a result. They would have to take math, tuition will go up for them, and graduation might end up delayed. These results are definitely not what anyone wants. Forcing math courses on everyone is not the answer. To improve the math skills of students who need help, colleges and universities should take another approach: they should assess incoming students to determine their needs, design effective courses to meet these needs, and re-assess the results each term to improve these courses. By taking a more balanced approach is a better idea for colleges and universities.

   b) Exchange your work with a partner and discuss how you have corrected the problems with modification and parallelism that you identified in part (a).

8. Go over an essay you have already written in this or another course. Are there any problems with modification or parallelism that you can find? If so, fix them. If you have been working on the essay assigned in the activity sequence of Modules 1.6 to 1.8, you will want to apply what you've learned in this module to identify and correct any problems with modification and faulty parallelism. Pay careful attention to any lists of points that you use in your introduction and conclusion.

Wordiness

[MODULE **2.7**]

Wordiness

Module Objectives

Upon successful completion of this module, you should be able to

1. define the terms *wordy* and *concise*

2. explain the importance of concise writing for both post-secondary and workplace/professional writing

3. recognize wordy constructions

4. apply specific techniques for reducing wordiness, including

   a) eliminating general redundancy
   b) eliminating empty "filler" words/phrases
   c) rewording verb + noun constructions by converting nouns to verbs

5. revise sentences, both individually and in context, to eliminate wordiness without loss of meaning

---

Self-Check **1**

Read the module objectives above. You've probably encountered some of these terms and concepts before; others, however, will likely be new. In point form, identify what seems familiar and what seems new to you in the chart below.

What do I already know about the topics in this module's objectives?	What seems new to me?

Wordy vs. Concise

Here's an actual example of a "wordy" sentence from the first draft of this book:

> One of the most common problems for beginning post-secondary students is wordy writing.

This sentence has 13 words. Here's a shorter version that says exactly the same thing:

> Wordy writing is a common problem for beginning post-secondary students.

This sentence has 10 words.

Imagine a flooded basement. You can't do anything or see anything properly because of the water and muck obscuring the space. Like water, extra words flood sentences: they make them difficult to read and difficult to understand.

Extra words also make it harder to get a good grade because your teacher does not enjoy reading five pages of material that communicates only three pages of actual meaningful content.

To make your writing more effective, you have to pump the sludge of out your sentences. This module is all about how to do just that.

Unlike flooded basements, wordy sentences tend to occur naturally in drafts. Even very experienced writers produce wordy sentences. When drafting, writers sometimes like to focus on getting the words down on paper. This approach is fine so long as the writer takes the time to eliminate wordiness later in the writing process.

One important trick is recognizing wordy sentences. The other trick is learning to make them shorter.

What, exactly, is wordiness, anyway? And what is conciseness?

Wordy writing uses more words than necessary to express an idea. Concise writing, the opposite, uses the minimum number of words necessary to express the idea.

What is the minimum number of words, though? It depends on what you want to say. Let's return to the example above:

> One of the most common problems for beginning post-secondary students is wordy writing.

The key words in this sentence are *wordy writing, common problem,* and *beginning post-secondary students.* We also need a verb to link these words together.

The first phrase *wordy writing* is crucial because that's the main topic of the sentence. The phrase *common problem* is crucial because it's also a key point. *Post-secondary students* is key because it explains who has the problem.

You might think for a second about the word *beginning*: this word is also important because the distinction is between beginning students and more advanced ones. Thus, deleting *beginning* would change the meaning.

The initial sentence has more words, though: *one of the most.* The expression *one of the* isn't really necessary here. While the revised version doesn't say that wordiness is the only common problem, its wording acknowledges that there might be others, but the others aren't really part of the current discussion. The phrase *one of the* can go.

The word *most* is trickier. The question to ask here is this: is it important for the argument that the problem under discussion is the "most common"? Does the writer, for example, compare how common this problem is relative to another?

If yes, the word *most* might be important. Here, however, the point is that the problem is common, so the word *most* can go.

The revised version also turns the sentence around so that it begins with the phrase *wordy writing.* Once you reverse the order and delete the unnecessary words, you get the revised version, which has three fewer words than the original.

Three words may not seem like a lot, but imagine if you could reduce every sentence in a long document by three words. Or you could think of it this way: 3 out of 13 is 23 per cent, so the second version is a significant 23 per cent shorter than the original.

The deleted words are empty in the sense that they add no meaning. Sometimes writers use such empty words as filler to make their sentences longer by stretching out the meaning across more words. Such stretching is not a good thing, but to explain why, we need to ask a bigger question: why should writers write concisely in the first place?

Concise writing has many advantages, as the following table explains:

Advantage	Explanation
Concise writing communicates more efficiently.	Concise writing allows readers to figure out the writer's meaning by reading fewer words. You can also think about the situation in reverse: by forcing readers to read more words than is necessary to convey the writer's meaning, a wordy writer is arguably wasting the reader's time.
	With regard to the example above, another way of thinking of a 23 per cent reduction in the word count is as a 23 per cent reduction in the reader's *workload*.
Concise writers have more room to add more points, more examples, more evidence, and so on.	Just as readers usually have limited time, writers usually have limited space.
	Such limits exist in courses in terms of word counts on papers. They also exist in the workplace because employers do not have unlimited resources: there are only so many hours in a day.
Concise writing helps you get higher marks.	This point follows from the point above: more content usually equals more marks, assuming that the writing is also good. The reverse is also true: very wordy writing will result in lower marks because your teachers are experienced readers who will in most cases be turned off by wordy writing.
Concise writing helps you get more done at work.	This point also follows from above: because concise writing is more efficient, you will save time at work. Imagine a supervisor with two employees. One produces wordy writing that takes a long time to read. The other produces concise writing that does not. No one likes having time wasted.

For all of these reasons, concise writing is good writing.

Wordy Habits and How to Break Them

In some ways, there are as many ways to eliminate wordiness as there are sentences. There are, however, some common habits that cause writers to write wordy sentences. Fortunately, like other bad habits, you can break them. The result will be better, more concise writing.

Identify and Eliminate Redundancy

Perhaps at some point you've seen a joke sign that reads

This joke provides the definition of redundancy: when something is redundant, it's unnecessary. Something else is doing the job, and the job does not need to be done twice.

Writers often pack unnecessary words into their writing. That's fine, so long as they cut them out when they edit. Given that you don't always have time to edit, though, it's best to try to get into the habit of avoiding redundancy in the first place.

Here are some examples of redundancy in writing:

In today's society, many people are concerned about the economy.

The opening phrase in the sentence above is redundant. The sentence uses the verb *are*, the present tense, which means today. It cannot mean anything other than today (as opposed to the past or the future). Similar problems happen with words like *today* or *nowadays*. Although they are sometimes necessary, they often aren't. If you don't need them, strike them out.

Consider this other example:

> Taking illegal drugs can harm a person's health and reputation. [10 words]

The word *taking* here is unnecessary, unless the writer is making a distinction between taking them and doing something else with them (selling them, etc.). Unless such is the case, you can rewrite as follows:

> Illegal drugs can harm a person's health and reputation. [9 words]

Note: You might even be tempted to go further here and delete *health and reputation*, resulting in this sentence:

> Illegal drugs can harm a person. [6 words]

However, as *health* and *reputation* add more specific information about exactly what the illegal drugs harm, deleting these words will result in loss of meaning. If you think the words add necessary information, leave them in the sentence.

Avoid Wordy Phrases

Some phrases are inherently wordy: they are almost always empty, providing nothing but filler. A classic example is this one:

> **Because**
> **Due to the fact that my power went out last night, my alarm didn't go off this morning.**

The problem with *due to the fact that* is this: why use five words when there is a single word—*because*—that means exactly the same thing?

You may also be wondering about the phrases *last night* and *this morning*. Unlike the example in the previous section, these phrases are actually necessary for the sentence's meaning, so they should stay.

Other common sources of wordiness include the phrases *there is/there are*. Although these phrases can help writers vary their structure, they add extra words:

> There are several problems with his argument. [7 words]

You can't reword this sentence just be deleting words; however, if you rearrange it slightly, you can write

> His argument has several problems. [5 words]

Change Nouns to Verbs When Possible

Consider this sentence:

> The writer draws a comparison between the two positions. [9 words]

If you think about the phrase *draws a comparison*, you will probably realize that *comparison* is a noun that you can turn into a verb. If you turn *comparison* into a verb, you don't actually need the verb *draws*, and you end up with this sentence:

> The writer compares the two positions. [6 words]

By using the verb form of the noun, you can trim three words from the sentence.

This particular problem is extremely common: writers use a verb plus a noun or a noun that can be a verb when there is actually a single verb that means the same thing as the wordier verb + noun version. Why use several words when you can use one? You can usually trim several words from a sentence by following the advice in this section.

Recap

Wordy habits	Examples and explanation	Solution
Redundancy	Some words/phrases are unnecessary because they add information that other parts of the sentence provide:	Delete the redundant words:
	In today's society, many people are concerned about the economy. [10 words]	Many people are concerned about the economy. [7 words]
Inherently wordy phrases	Some phrases take the long way around by using several words to express an idea that fewer words can express:	Use a more concise expression/word that means the same thing:
	Due to the fact that Lemner provides no evidence, his argument is not credible. [14 words]	Because Lemner provides no evidence, his argument is not credible. [10 words]

Wordy habits	Examples and explanation	Solution
Using nouns that can be turned into verbs	Some nouns can also be verbs, and using the noun version requires a separate, unnecessary verb: The security guard asked the students questions. [7 words]	Go directly to the appropriate verb. If there is a noun that you can change into a verb, do so: The security guard questioned the students. [6 words]

Module Checklist

Have I

- ☐ checked my sentences for redundancy?
- ☐ eliminated filler words/phrases?
- ☐ reworded verb + noun constructions as verbs, when possible?

Looking Ahead

Sludgy, wordy sentences don't work well in any writing, whether for a class assignment or for a job application or work assignment, so wherever and whenever you write anything, the advice here works.

In the shorter term, however, the material in this module also leads into Module 2.8: Editing, Revising, and Proofreading. This next module combines material from the entire book.

Although we have dealt with separate topics module by module for the sake of convenience, when you actually write in the real world, you need to deal with everything at once. The last module in Part 2 helps you practise doing so.

Self-Check 2

Refer back to the first self-check at the beginning of this module. Have your ideas changed? What new ideas do you have? Write them out in the chart below.

Based on the objectives at the start, how have my views changed since the beginning of this module?	What new information do I have?

Activities

Before turning to the next module, check your understanding of the concepts and terms of this module by completing the activities below.

1. a) Write out (on either paper or computer) any wordy phrases or expressions that you can think of that are not covered in this module.

    b) Add to the list that you have created in 1(a) by Googling *wordy phrases*. Which additional phrases did you find that were not on your list or in this module? Write them down along with any suggestions for making them more concise.

    c) Compare your list with a classmate's. Discuss how you would fix each of the phrases that you have written on your lists.

2. The following table contains wordy sentences. Complete the chart by first identifying the cause of the wordiness, based on what you have learned in this module. Then, revise the sentences to eliminate the wordiness. Count the words in your revised versions.

Wordy sentence	Cause of wordiness	Revised version (give word count)
a) Saputo makes a connection between Smith's education and training as a lawyer and his writing style. [16 words]		
b) Crandall places heavy emphasis on Saputo's lack of statistical evidence. [10 words]		
c) There is a design principle today that using a bold font provides effective emphasis of the key elements. [18 words]		
d) Better instruction about quotation, paraphrase, and summary will create a reduction in plagiarism cases at our school. [17 words]		
e) I have had the opportunity to take several writing classes. [10 words]		
f) There is a useful analysis of that topic in this article. [11 words]		
g) Kaprov issues a challenge to Cook's claim that his proposal will create a reduction in costs. [16 words]		

3. With a partner, exchange your answers to Activity 2 above and discuss.

4. Rewrite the following paragraph to make it more concise:

> Zacarias' entire proposal is logically dependent on two ideas: that students are immature and that a "gap year" would have benefits for students. The main benefit, she argues, would be improved academic performance because of greater maturity. There are several serious problems with her argument here. One of these problems is that she provides yet another example of a common tendency to overgeneralize about students' immaturity on a regular basis. Another problem involves her evidence. Due to the fact that she cites no research showing that a "gap year" would result in improvements to students' academic performance, her proposal is not justified. Her entire argument here is an example of poor use of evidence. Colleges and universities should conduct careful analysis on the benefits and drawbacks of any proposal before agreeing to it. [133 words]

5. With a partner, compare your rewritten versions of the paragraph from Activity 4. How are they similar? How are they different?

6. Review examples of your own writing, either for this class or for another one. Find examples of wordiness and rewrite the sentences to make them more concise.

Editing, Revising, and Proofreading

[MODULE **2.8**]

Editing, Revising, and Proofreading

Module Objectives

Upon successful completion of this module, you will be able to

1. define the terms *edit*, *revise*, and *proofread*

2. identify general and personal strategies for editing, revising, and proofreading

3. create a personal editing inventory identifying particular areas to monitor in your own writing

4. apply these general and personal strategies for editing, revising, and proofreading to a variety of texts

---

Self-Check **1**

Read the module objectives above. You've probably encountered some of these terms and concepts before; others, however, will likely be new. In point form, identify what seems familiar and what seems new to you in the chart below.

What do I already know about the topics in this module's objectives?	What seems new to me?

I Have a Draft—Now What?

Consider the following rough draft:

> I don't think students should have to do math. In the artical,
> "Future=Math," by the author May Agnesi she argues that college
> students need math in today's society because their jobs need
> math, like even servers in restaurants need to make change,
> other jobs require math to, especially things like engineers
> and computers. May makes the proposal that all students be
> required to take math courses. Her proposal is an
> overgeneralization.
>
> According to May: students can't do basic things with math like
> do percents, or figure out grades. Because they need math for
> the future: this is a big problem. She doesn't give evidence,
> though so it's not proof that students cant math therefore I
> don't think her proposal can go too far as she wants to go. Also,
> its not fair to treat everyone the same like she overgeneralizes
> about them, some students hate math more than anything and
> some like it and are good with what she says and different kinds
> of students need different math anyway. Any individual student
> in a big group of students are different, maybe, and Agnesi
> ignores it. They might fail or not graduate or take longer, which
> is expensive for them with tuition going up. Some students are
> too poor to pay extra for math courses.
>
> Agnesi should redo her proposal so its less ridiculous.

The term *draft*, in fact, refers to an unfinished version of a piece of writing. We use the term *rough draft* here because this piece of writing needs a lot of work.

Although it has an introduction, a body, and a conclusion, and although it begins to make some good points about Agnesi's proposal, the writing above has a lot of problems. These problems are of several different sorts. In fact, if you review the advice about writing in this book, you'll see that the writer here hasn't followed most of it.

Sometimes writers simply need to get their main ideas and structure down in this kind of basic, rough form. Once a rough draft exists, however, more work follows. This extra work involves a set of closely related activities: *editing*, *revising*, and *proofreading*.

This module defines these terms and also provides some fairly specific suggestions about how to apply them, both to this sample and to writing more generally.

Editing, Revising, and Proofreading: What Are They?

There can be a lot of confusion about the terms *editing*, *revising*, and *proofreading*, so let's begin with short dictionary definitions of each one. *The Concise Oxford Canadian Dictionary* defines each term as follows:

Term	Definition
When you **edit**, you	"reword, revise, or alter (a text, etc.) to correct, alter the emphasis."
When you **revise**, you	"examine or re-examine and improve" a piece of writing.
When you **proofread**, you	"read . . . and mark any errors."

Based on these definitions, editing and revising seem like very similar activities. In fact, the definition for *edit* uses the verb *revise*. For the rest of this module, we are going to use the term *revising*. However, you should know that some people will also use the term *editing*, so if you encounter it, it refers to the same kinds of processes for making improvements as *revising*.

Proofreading, in contrast, is a more limited, more focused activity. Although editing and revising are relatively open-ended processes of reading and making improvements to a piece of writing, proofreading is a much narrower process that involves fixing grammatical mistakes, misspellings, and typos.

Sometimes it helps to think of proofreading as focusing on the surface presentation of your writing, while revising focuses on the deeper aspects of your work: argument, structure, precision, clarity, and so on.

As we'll explain in greater detail below, revising happens before proofreading, which is usually the final activity involving a piece of writing before you submit it. At the proofreading stage, you really should only be fixing surface errors like typos and misspellings and minor grammatical problems, not making deeper changes to content, organization, or sentence structure.

While proofreading, if you find yourself adding more material, doing substantial rewriting, and so on, you are still in the revision stage of your essay writing, and you're not quite ready for proofreading yet.

We should also note, though, that proofreading doesn't necessarily happen only once. For example, professional writers proofread before they submit drafts to their publishers, and the publishers send these drafts back with comments and suggestions, and the whole process can start over again. In other words, these different categories can occur repeatedly in different stages, especially in writing intended for publication.

The Big Myth about Writing

Good, polished, insightful writing very rarely just happens. This observation points to a common myth about writing. Some people believe that good writers magically put words on screen and page, and that raw talent alone makes the writing good the first time around.

Highly skilled writers will usually produce better first drafts than less-skilled ones do, true, but all writing, even writing done by highly skilled, experienced writers, benefits from careful reflection, revision, and proofreading. In fact, although the writers of this book are all English professors with decades of experience teaching the topics in this book, the paragraph you're reading right now has been frequently and extensively revised.

If you had an opportunity to see the many drafts of each module that this book went through, you'd immediately notice a very large number of changes, including additions, deletions, rewording, format changes, and various other changes.

Rewriting early drafts several times does not mean that you're a bad writer; it means that you're following the correct process. Writing is often *re*writing.

Depending on the situation, you will have more or less time to work on your writing. If you're writing an in-class essay or exam essay, for example, you won't have time to work through several drafts.

On the other hand, in out-of-class essays, your teachers will usually give you the topics well in advance, and if you start early, you will have more time to follow the advice given here so that you can make your writing as good as it can be.

Time alone, however, isn't enough. Imagine if you had to build a house but didn't really have any knowledge of house design or construction. Having extra time isn't going to help you all that much in this situation—what you need is time *plus* specific knowledge.

That's where the rest of this module comes into play: editing and revising (whichever term you're using) are most effective when you know what to look for in terms of specific areas for improvement. It is thus an open-ended activity with some fairly specific elements.

Your Personal Inventory

An inventory is a record of what is present and what is missing. When businesses take inventory, they count everything they have in stock and thus identify items that need replacing. However, we are using this word in a different (though related) sense: a personal writing inventory involves recording both the writing skills you have and the writing skills that you need to develop further.

Everyone has different strengths and weaknesses as a writer: some people are especially good at summarizing but have more trouble coming up with their own arguments. Others are especially good at organizing their ideas but have more trouble with grammar and punctuation.

Whatever your strengths and weaknesses, you should take advantage of your strengths when you can but also identify your weaknesses and make an effort to improve in these areas.

Instead of ignoring your areas for improvement, or hoping that they will improve on their own, a better strategy involves being on the lookout for them and keeping track of them—in other words, taking an inventory.

Such an inventory can take whatever form you find most convenient, but we would suggest an easy-to-read checklist format like the ones we have placed at the end of all of the modules in this book.

So, for example, if you have trouble with topic sentences (see page 102 in Module 1.7), you should pay particular attention to this area as you edit and revise your work. If you tend to misspell certain words (see the table beginning on page 262 of this module), you should keep track of them somewhere and take extra care to ensure that they are correct when you proofread.

Your teacher may also ask you to prepare an inventory of your areas for improvement as a course activity or assignment, and if so, you should follow any instructions carefully with regard to formatting and presentation. For example, your teacher may want you to arrange your inventory as a checklist, a table, or some other way. When in doubt, ask your teacher.

Proofreading

Once you think the content, structure, and other deep features are set, you are ready to proofread. The best way to proofread is to read your writing out loud to yourself. For this reason, we suggest that you don't proofread in a public place.

Reading out loud forces your eye and brain to pause on every word, and as your mouth forms the word, you gain another layer of perception to notice problems. How often have you ever been reading something and noticed that you've left out a word in the middle of a sentence? Reading out loud helps you see—and fix—such problems.

Sometimes you think you're ready to proofread, and then you find yourself making more substantial changes—adding examples, changing the order of the sentences, rewriting entire sentences, and so on. If that happens, keep going, but be aware that you're not proofreading—you're revising. Every time you make deeper changes, you need to proofread again after you've made them, as changes can cause new mistakes to creep into your work.

You know you're finished proofreading when you have read the entire document out loud and made no changes at all. Until then, you're not done.

Problem Words

Below you will find a table outlining some words that may give you problems when you are writing. We've focused on frequently confused words.

However, you may notice that *you* have a particular word that you sometimes confuse with a different word that isn't on this list. When you discover a word that gives you trouble, you should look up the definition of that word, and write an example sentence using the word correctly. Keep this sentence handy for future reference. Over time, you will create an easy-to-use, personalized list, tailored to your own writing.

If you build on this table with some words of your own, you will have a valuable tool to help you when it comes to proofreading your work.

Problem word	Confused with	Notes	Example of correct use
a lot	alot	"Alot" is not a word. The correct version is *a lot* (two words).	There are **a lot** of problems with Zacarias' arguments.
affect (verb)	effect (verb)	The most common meaning of *affect* as a verb is "to influence." Note: *Affect* can also be a noun, but unless you're taking psychology, this usage of the word will rarely come up, so for now, we won't worry about it.	This bad weather negatively **affects** my mood.

Problem word	Confused with	Notes	Example of correct use
although	althoug	"Althoug" is not a word. The correct spelling is *although*.	**Although** Agnesi makes some good points about the importance of math, her generalizations about students are unacceptable.
article	artical	An article is a short piece of writing, often in essay format. "Artical" is incorrect: there is no such word in English.	A published **article** can be convincing evidence for arguments.
defiantly	definitely	*Defiantly* is an adverb meaning "in an oppositional manner." *Definitely* is an adverb meaning "certainly," "without a doubt," etc.	He **defiantly** continued with his flawed proposal, despite all reasonable criticisms of it.
definitely	defiantly	See above.	There are **definitely** problems with the argument; however, these problems can be solved with more research.
effect (noun)	affect (noun)	*Effect* as a noun means "a resulting change." It can also be a verb meaning "to cause."	This bad weather has a negative **effect** on my mood.
effect (verb)	affect (verb)	*Effect* as a verb means "to cause."	The Internet has **effected** great change.
loose (adjective)	lose	*Loose* as an adjective means the opposite of tight: "poorly connected," "scattered," "incoherent." *Lose* is a verb meaning "to suffer loss," "to no longer possess something."	The car's front wheel is **loose**. The structure of the argument is very **loose** and thus hard to follow.

(Continued)

Problem word	Confused with	Notes	Example of correct use
lose (verb)	Loose (verb) or loose (adjective).	*Lose* is a verb meaning "to suffer a loss, to no longer possess something." *Loose* is a verb meaning "to release." Regarding *loose* as an adjective, see above.	Problems with evidence will cause a writer to **lose** credibility.
than	then	*Than* is used for comparisons. (*Then* refers to time.)	The revised essay is much better **than** the rough draft.
their	there, they're	*Their* is the possessive of *they. There*, in contrast, refers to place, as in "over there"; it also appears in expressions like *there is/are. They're* is a contraction—a short form—of *they are*.	My sister and her husband are renovating **their** house.
there	their, they're	See above.	**There** are several other practical solutions to this problem.
they're	their, there	See above.	**They're** arriving at 7:00 tonight.
then	than	*Then* indicates when in time something occurred. *Then* is also a transition word meaning next or consequently. (*Than* is used for comparisons.)	I will see you **then**. This change, **then**, would negatively affect students.
you're	your	*You're* is a contraction meaning "you are." *Your* is a possessive adjective, indicating "something belonging to you."	**You're** a very good writer.
your	you're	See above.	**Your** writing has improved a great deal.

Module Checklist

Each module so far has featured a Module Checklist at the end to remind you of key areas of improvement in your writing. Now it's time to create your own personal checklist—in other words, a personal writing inventory.

Activities 1 and 2 for this module are all about creating this checklist. Our hope is that you will identify the particular problems that you face when you sit down to write or revise an essay.

If you put some time into this personal inventory, you'll have an excellent writing tool that is customized just for you.

Looking Ahead

This module pulls together material from the entire book—when you revise and proofread, you will use all the knowledge and strategies you have learned from the beginning of the book until now.

For example, revision will require you to focus on paragraph cohesion, the use of evidence, strong thesis claims, and meaningful conclusions. Proofreading will require you to use the skills you've developed to fix grammatical errors, misspellings, and frequently confused words.

A well-revised, properly proofread essay will help to give you credibility with your readers and might be the tipping point in persuading them of your point of view.

As we have pointed out throughout, though, the skills you have developed here are not the end of the line: in additional courses you will learn new writing skills that build on the ones here.

Writing well is a process, and each situation is different. You should continue to keep and develop the kind of personal writing inventory that we have described in this module, either as a formal document or, at the very least, a set of mental habits. Good luck!

Self-Check 2

Refer back to the first self-check at the beginning of this module. Have your ideas changed? What new ideas do you have? Write them out in the chart below.

Based on the objectives at the start, how have my views changed since the beginning of this module?	What new information do I have?

Activities

Check your understanding of the concepts and terms of this module by completing the activities below.

1. As we suggested above in the Module Checklist section, it's now time to construct a checklist of your own. Prepare a personal inventory of your strengths and weaknesses as a writer based on your experiences with the other modules in this book. What areas do you tend to be good at? What things do you need to especially watch for as you compose, revise, and proofread your own work?

2. Exchange your inventory and a sample of your writing with a partner and compare. Based on each partner's writing sample, do you have any advice for each other regarding strategies/techniques for improvement? Make revisions based on your partner's suggestions.

    Note: Your teacher may wish you to submit a copy of your personal inventory, so pay careful attention to his or her instructions about how the checklist should be organized, formatted, and so on.

3. Look again at the short essay that opens this module (on page 257) and improve it. To do so, apply all the advice from this module and all the specific points from all of the other modules in this book.

    You should use the Module Checklists from the other modules in this book to help you with the revision process. Remember that many mistakes become easier to find if you read the text aloud.

4. Exchange your revision of the short essay with a partner, and compare what you have done. Your improvements won't always be exactly the same. Did you miss anything your partner noticed? You may wish to add things that you missed to the personal inventory that you created in Activities 1 and 2.

5. Your teacher will give a fresh essay topic that you haven't written about yet. Write a rough draft, and then apply all the advice from this module to your draft: the result should be a carefully revised and proofread essay. Your teacher will give you more detailed instructions about exactly what you should do.

    Your teacher may also ask you to apply the revision and proofreading techniques discussed here to the model essay that you've been working through in the activities in Modules 1.6 through 1.8.

Appendix A

Conjunctions

1. Coordinating Conjunctions

for
and
nor
but
or
yet
so

2. Subordinating Conjunctions

Here is a list of subordinating conjunctions that you can use in your writing. There are others, but these are the most important ones to know in relation to the writing topics covered in this book.

after	if only	that
although	inasmuch	the first time
as	in case	though
as if	in order that	unless
as long as	in the event that	until
as soon as	just in case	what
as though	lest	whatever
because	now that	when
before	once	whenever
by the time	only if	whereas
even if	provided that	wherever
even though	since	whether (or not)
ever since	so that	which
every time	than	while
if		

Conjunctive Adverbs and Transitions

accordingly	furthermore	nevertheless
additionally	hence	next
after this	henceforth	nonetheless
afterward	however	now
also	if not	on the contrary
anyway	indeed	on the other hand
as a result	instead	otherwise
besides	in addition	rather
certainly	in comparison	similarly
comparatively	in contrast	still
consequently	in fact	subsequently
conversely	in short	that is
elsewhere	in the meantime	then
equally	later	thereafter
finally	likewise	therefore
for example	meanwhile	thus
for this reason	moreover	undoubtedly
further	namely	

Appendix C

Indefinite Pronouns

1. **Almost Always Singular**
   Type A (words ending in *-one*, *-body*, or *-thing*)

anybody	everyone	nothing
anyone	everything	somebody
anything	nobody	someone
everybody	no one	something

   Type B

another	much
each	neither
either	one
little	other

2. **Always Plural**

both	others
few	several
many	

3. **Can Be Singular or Plural Depending on the Context**

all	most
any	none
more	some

Index

Credits

LITERARY CREDITS

31 Graff, Gerald, and Cathy Birkenstein. *They Say/I Say: The Moves That Matter in Academic Writing*. 2nd ed. New York: W.W. Norton & Company, Inc., 2009.

35 National Geographic, *Guide to the National Parks of Canada*. Washington, D.C.: The National Geographic Society, 2011.

45 "The Tangerine Factor." *The Big Bang Theory*, 2008. Reproduced with permission of Warner Bros. Television.

54 & 60 Dictionary definitions adapted from *Concise Canadian Oxford Dictionary*. Don Mills, ON: Oxford University Press, 2005.

142 Quotation from Carr, Nicholas. "Is Google Making Us Stupid?" *The Atlantic*. July/August 2008.

258 Dictionary definitions adapted from *Concise Canadian Oxford Dictionary*. Don Mills, ON: Oxford University Press, 2005.

PHOTO CREDITS

45 © Gruffi/Shutterstock
49 © Vanzyst/Shutterstock

248 © Fulop Zsolt/Shutterstock;
257 © tomgigabite/Shutterstock